PRAISE

"J. R. Solonche can pack so much humor and linguistic playfulness into such tight bundles, it feels like 1,000 clowns issuing from a VW Bug. He can also fit a lot of darkness and mortality into them, which feels more like 1,000 clowns dressed like Marilyn Mason issuing from a VW Bug. Solonche can be crass the way only the truthful can be, mischievous as a child with his hands in the honey jar, or even aphoristic and proverbial like a modern day Martial. Though you never know which Solonche you're going to encounter on the next page, he's a great bunch of guys to get to know."

> —STEPHEN CRAMER, winner of the Louise Bogan Award and the National Poetry Series

"The poems of J. R. Solonche catch the reader off-guard in playful profundity. While always mindful of the tradition of poetry masquerading as direct statement (the like of W. C. Williams, Robert Bly, Robert Creeley, and Charles Bukowski), J. R. Solonche nevertheless 'makes it new' through his masterful use of understatement, aphorism, word play and anaphora—raising poem after thoughtful poem from the familiar and often overlooked 'little things' of the poet's day-to-day encounter with the world."

> —PHILLIP STERLING, author of *And Then Snow*

"In a style that favors brevity and pith, J. R. Solonche brings a richness of experience, observation, and wit into his poems. Here is the world! they exclaim. And here and here and here! Watched over by ancient lyric gods—Time, Death, and Desire—we find the quotidian here transformed."

> —CHRISTOPHER NELSON, editor of Green Linden Press

"Solonche, an accomplished poet, employs various forms in this compilation, including haiku, prose poem, and free verse. The poems often imaginatively enter into the natural or material world via anthropomorphic similes...Many works have an aphoristic quality that recall Zen koans, and they can be playfully amusing or even silly...A strong set of sympathetic but never sentimental observations."

"These short poems are an extraordinary amalgam of wit, close observation, humor, and clear-seeing. Each one singles out and illuminates an ordinary moment—ordinary, that is, until the poet explodes into a miniature epiphany. Easy of access and frequently profound, J. R. Solonche's poems induce in me a state of delighted surprise."

"The history of book blurbs is littered with high falutin' praise, whacky and wild metaphors, written to impress not to inform. All I need to say about J. R. Solonche's poems is that they are good, really, really good. So much so that they have a high "I-wish-I'd-written-that" factor. That's a compliment I hand out to very few poets writing today. You want wit? You want humor? You want erudition? You want them all mixed into poems? Try Solonche. You won't be disappointed. Envious perhaps, but not disappointed."

COLLECTED SHORT POEMS

J. R. SOLONCHE

INTRODUCTION BY
AMANDA HOLMES DUFFY

SHANTI ARTS PUBLISHING
BRUNSWICK, MAINE

COLLECTED SHORT POEMS

Published by Shanti Arts Publishing

Designed by Shanti Arts Designs

Cover image by FREEPIK

Shanti Arts LLC
193 Hillside Road
Brunswick, Maine 04011

shantiarts.com

Printed in the United States of America

ISBN: 978-1-962082-68-6 (print, softcover)

LCCN: 2025936448

TITLES BY THIS AUTHOR

POETRY
The Consolations
Barren Road
Night Visit
Old
Then Morning
Reading Takuboku Ishikawa
The Architect's House
God
The Eglantine
Alone
The Dreams of the Gods
The Book of a Small Fisherman
Leda
It's about Time
Around Here
The Lost Notebook of Zhao Li
Coming To
Life-Size
The Five Notebooks of Zhao Li
Selected Poems 2002-2021
Years Later
The Dust
A Guide of the Perplexed
For All I Know
The Moon Is the Capital of the World
Piano Music
Enjoy Yourself
The Time of Your Life
The Porch Poems
To Say the Least
A Public Place

(continued)

True Enough
If You Should See Me Walking on the Road
I, Emily Dickinson and Other Found Poems
The Jewish Dancing Master
Tomorrow, Today and Yesterday
In Short Order
Invisible
Heart's Content
Won't Be Long
Beautiful Day
Peach Girl: Poems for a Chinese Daughter (with Joan I. Siegel)

CRITICISM
An Aesthetic Toward Notes: On Poets & Poetry

CONTENTS

from **THE BLACK BIRCH** (2017)

A PLACE FOR THE GENUINE
— ON READING J. R. SOLONCHE —

Introduction by
AMANDA HOLMES DUFFY

Not long ago, I was enjoying some light conversation with friends over dinner when the discussion turned to poetry, a subject that consumes much of my time. Nearly every day I read it, write about it, read it aloud to myself, and record it on my podcast. But why is it important? Sandra asked me. She didn't understand, because apart from charming little verses like "Twinkle twinkle little star," she finds poetry boring.

In the moment, I rose to poetry's defense. I also felt a little sad. I didn't admit it at the time, but part of me knew what she meant. Sandra enjoyed nursery rhymes as her earliest experience of poetry, but more developed and contemporary forms leave her unmoved. J. R. Solonche knows this, too, for he asks a similar question:

> Iell me again
> what I was told
>
> when I was young
> what poetry is
>
> supposed to do.
> I am old.
>
> I am old.
> I have forgotten.

I'm reminded of Karl Ove Knausgaard's comments on poetry in Book 2 of *My Struggle*: "I could read it, but poems never opened themselves to me, and that was because I had no 'right' to them: they were not for me. When I approached them, I felt like a fraud, and was indeed always unmasked because what they always said was, 'Who do you think you are, coming here?'"

Even Marianne Moore, that supreme craftsman, opens "Poetry" with the admission: "I too dislike it." But she then drills into the core of poetry, exploring what it does and why it matters. Her assessment includes what we as children love without question: discovering those "imaginary gardens with real toads in them," and finding in poetry "a place for the genuine."

Solonche is nothing if not genuine. He can paint a picture or sum up a mood in a few broad strokes. He can be joyful, reflective, or wry, but he's always mindful of the absurdities in life, and he never leaves his reader behind. When he plays with words, you want to join in too.

I laughed out loud when I read "Any Poem by John Ashbery":

> Where poetry
> goes when it
> wants to be
> alone.

Though we may enjoy Ashbery from time to time, I think even the most dedicated readers will agree that the insular nature of much contemporary poetry can be off-putting. It can jump through hoops, leaving prosody and lyricism behind—thus leaving us behind as well.

Solonche frequently addresses other poets in his work, admires them, has learned from them, knows how to dig deep with them, and sometimes calls them out. Who could disagree with his assessment of *Beowulf*?

> Yes, it is long,
> Yes, it is boring.
> But, holy shit,
> it's the greatest
> long, boring
> poem there is.

His critique of poetry is also grounded in an appreciation of the sacred wisdom of children, which poets as well as readers often leave behind them as they age. He writes "In the Georgia O'Keeffe Museum, Santa Fe":

> I asked my eight-year-old
> daughter what she thought
> of *Part of the Cliffs* and of
> the photograph of the site
> for *Part of the Cliffs*, which
> was on the wall next to it.
> "The photograph is what
> she saw with her eyes open.
> The painting is what she saw
> with her eyes closed," she said.

And in another poem:

> After the reading, the poet
> was asked, "Why do you write?"
> "I write because the silence is
> too much to bear," he answered.
> I hope someone asks me the same
> question, for I shall answer, "I write
> because the noise is too much to bear."

Yes, when reading poetry, we can often have enough of words. But Solonche is never wordy. He never rambles. Never pads. Never indulges himself with words.

And let's not forget the simple beauty of his imagist poems. The pictures he paints come at you so clearly you forget you are reading, much like A. R. Ammons, another poet he admires. Lakes and trees, birds, butterflies, and bees—nature figures strongly in Solonche's work, yet it is never sentimental. He gets out of his own way and in so doing, gets out of our way too, as seen in "The Lake in the Rain":

> The lake in the rain
> remembers when it was
> the rain and quietly cries
> in the depths of its sleep,
> which, if you carefully
> listen, sounds like rain
> on a lake.

When I read Solonche, I expect to have some fun. But his work is not without sorrow. He can break your heart a little, but he bears his sorrows lightly. I find myself mulling over some pieces, returning to them, finding in them keys to the human condition, to what it means to endure. As in "Dementia":

> "Does she still smile?"
> her friend asked.
> "Yes, she still smiles,"
> I said. "I think she
> will always smile,"
> she said. "Yes, the
> doctor thinks so too,
> but he said the reasons
> will change," I said.

The book in your hands is a thick one but reading it you'll come away lighter. Poems can be like chocolates, especially when they're read aloud: too many at once and you feel a bit sick. Not so here. You will be sated, but uplifted, heartened, and companioned.

In a poem written to poet Ted Kooser he writes:

> Ted, you say your
> poem about your
> dead parents is dark.
> I say you do darkness
> with a light touch
> so the rest of us
> may see better in it.

One could say the same of Solonche. I admire his lightness of touch, his lack of pretention and his commitment to simplicity, especially when life feels complicated. He pares things down and never over-faces you.

I'll be sending a copy of this book to my friend Sandra, and you can confidently share this book with those who think they dislike poetry, too. Yet you can also share it with poetry lovers, read it aloud, or read it to yourself. It will never ask you who you think you are, coming here. It will never pass judgement on you. It will simply invite you to come as you are.

AMANDA HOLMES DUFFY
poetry editor for the *Washington Independent Review of Books*, and host of *Read Me a Poem*
from *The American Scholar*

from **Won't Be Long** (2016)

PATRIOTISM

I don't own an American flag.
I never have.
I grew up in an apartment building in the Bronx.
Nobody owned a flag.
Now that I live on a road in the country,
all my neighbors fly the flag.
Except one.
Like them, he does have a flagpole
with a flag hanging on it
in front of his house.
But he says he isn't flying it.
He says he's lynching it.

PHYSICAL

The stethoscope, his cold third ear,
pressed against my chest, "Take
a breath," my physician says as
though offering me a box full of
his own collection of breaths, each
one better than any of mine. "Breathe
in, hold it," he says, so this one
I roll around in my mouth, such
a fine brandy of breath he has poured just for me.

TO MY DESK

I have faith in you.
I trust you not to reveal them, our secrets.
You are hard and stubborn and loyal.
I know you will never tell what you have overheard.
No, not even if they torture you,
burn you with cigarettes, cut you with razors,
or break, one at a time, so painfully slowly,
your smooth, slender legs.

TOUCH

> ... the last sense to fade at life's culmination

So is this how it will be, Death, when we finally
      get married?
I will not see your face when I lift your veil?
I will not hear you whisper my name?
I will not smell your breath on my face?
I will not taste the wine?
I will only feel your hand in mine,
your touch, for only as long as it takes to say, "I do"?

HIS NOSE ANSWERS DR. WILLIAMS

No, I cannot be decent.
No, I cannot reserve my ardors
for something less unlovely than that rank
odor of a passing spring.
Yes, I must taste everything!
Yes, I must know everything!
Yes, I must have a part in everything!
And don't worry, Doc.
Flossie will care for us if we continue in these ways.

BLUE BUTTERFLY

I was outside reading.
A blue butterfly settled on the table.
The opening and closing of its blue wings
looked like a small blue book opening and closing.
Then it looked like a blue eye opening and closing.
Then it looked like the blue book.
Then it looked like the blue eye.
Then the blue book.
The blue eye.

MARCH

It is warm.
The snow is melting fast.
All three feet of it.
The water rushes down
the gutter and out
into the snow still on the grass.
The water is a liquid knife
working fast through the snow.
Ah, surgeon of the hot hands,
how you save the life of life.

I WANT TO DIE LIKE A NAVAJO

I want to die like a Navajo.
I want to sign the poem,
"When that time comes
when my last breath leaves
me, I choose to die
in peace to meet Shi' dy' in."
Then, as I will no longer
be on Mother earth,
you may wash up,
take your corn pollen,
and go on with life.

THE PERFECT PLACE

The perfect place is not a piece of paper.
It is not a book.
The perfect place is an old wall,
but whitewashed new,
which the citizens come upon suddenly,
taken unawares as they turn the corner
of their crowded city,
out of the corner
of their eye.

FALSE SPRING

Don't you hate spring
when it is not?
When it sticks its nose
into winter's business?
Don't you hate sunshine
when it is disingenuous?
Don't you hate melt
when it doesn't go all the way?
Don't you hate lies
no matter who the liar is?

YOU NEVER KNOW WHICH RAIN

You never know which rain
will be the last of fall's rain.
But I'm sure it isn't today's rain.
It is too warm.
The maples aren't yet done.
The year needs to bleed some
more before doctor winter
arrives with his pure white bandages,
with his sterile needles filled with sleep.

TO SLEEP

Death's dwarf,
headstone headliner's warm up act,
what sort of fool do you take me for, pal?
While I each night entrust myself to you,
my head knee-deep in your lap,
I wait for eternity to wield,
behind your back, its ax,
light as the feather in your cap.

AS TO WHAT HE HAS DONE

As to what he has done and what he has not:
He has taught some things to some
but has left much more untaught to many more.
He has written some words
but has left many more unwritten.
Many nights has he not slept thinking,
"What does better mean?"

THE TRAIN

When the train begins, it is far away.
When the train ends, it is far away.
Only for a minute is the train close enough to hear.
But it is only then that the train is what far away
        sounds like.

ON THE WALL OF THE TIBETAN ARTS STORE

On the wall of the Tibetan arts store,
I saw a mask of myself.
"How much?" I asked.
"It costs your soul," said the owner.
I bought it, put it on and left.
I wear it all the time except at night.
While asleep.
Or not asleep.

GEORGIA O'KEEFFE, *CITY NIGHT*

It is not just in the lilies
and the irises and the shells.
It is also here, in the dark cleft,
the mysterious canyon of skyscrapers.
Eroticism ironed out, squared off, hurried.
Even here in the cool glowing clitoris of moon.

WALK

"Look, there's a deer skull," I said,
  pointing to the deer skull by the side of the road.
"Look, there's a beer skull," Jim said,
  pointing to the Coors can by the side of the road.

STAND PERFECTLY STILL

Stand perfectly still
beneath the wild cherry tree
toward the end of April,
when it opens its hands to let fall
the white blossoms petal by petal,
singly and in clusters,
and you will know what it means to be dizzy
while standing perfectly still.

THE FLOWERS AT NIGHT

The flowers at night are all the same.
And at night, the trees are all the same.
So too are the clouds at night the same.
Only the wind at night is different,
so different as it moans its secrets
to the unwilling who cannot turn away.

THE NAMES

One spelled Dickinson with an e.
Another spelled Eliot with two l's.
A third spelled Whitman without an h.
If nothing else, I said, spell the names right.
At least spell the names right.
If nothing else, I said. The fucking names.

WHO WHISPERED

Who whispered into the ear of
the wild cherry tree that it blushed
rosy pink for a whole week?
Who told it that ribald tale
of the old man and his young wife
that it burst out in such a white
belly laugh of blossoms?

MY DAUGHTER WANTS TO SIT IN THE SHADE

My daughter wants to sit in the shade.
My wife wants to sit in the sun.
We move the table half in shade, half in sun.
Problem solved.
Yin and yang, right?
Well, not exactly.
Yin, yang, and yin.
As I sit in both.

HEY

Hey, want to do
a good deed today?
Befriend a lonely
old poem.

POEM ON A NAPKIN

When the napkin is spread on my lap,
the poem is a map.
When the napkin is tucked in my shirt,
the poem is a flirt.
When the napkin wipes my lip,
the poem is a slip
of the tongue.

ACROSS

Across the street is a church
with a cross above the door
and another one on the roof
and glass crosses in all the windows.
So many crosses, I suppose
they want us never to forget
who the boss is.

THE HUMMINGBIRD

The hummingbird drinks from one impatiens,
then from another, and then from a third.
Finally, it goes to the feeder filled with sugar water,
hangs around but does not drink.
Why should we be insulted?
We also planted the impatiens there.

PRIVATE PROPERTY

There are 57,308,738
square miles of land in the world.
That's 36,677,592,320 acres.
As decreed by Map 16, Block 2,
Lots 3 and 4, I own 0.50 acres.
This comes to 1/73,355,104,640th
of the land in the world.
Keep out!

PHILOSOPHY

The Pythagoreans worshiped number.
They believed that fire was made of 24
right angled triangles surrounded by 4
equilateral triangles composed of 6
right angled triangles.
But they thought about such things
only after the water boiled for morning coffee.

ENGLISH

How can you say anything bad
about a language that lets you sing
"I've been beaten down for so long
Lawd, Lawd, I feel all beaten up"?

AESTHETICS

The maker of the door
is not concerned with the room
into which the door opens,
nor is he concerned with the hall
upon which the door closes.
These are the concerns
of the maker of the walls.

SKUNK

Good morning, dawn
of white striped sun-
rise, let you be now my moral model
for the world,
for the worst of us, skunk, animal
best black and white,
of a better world whose only evil
is an evil smell.

I ASKED THE GUY ON PURGATORY ROAD

I asked the guy on Purgatory Road
why on earth he built a house so close
to the railroad tracks up there.
"I grew up on Jerome Avenue in the Bronx,"
he said, which explained everything.

SPRING

When the days get longer,
the birds know it is time to sing.
There is something in the mind
of the bird that responds
to light's lengthening.
As to what that is,
biologists are still in the dark.

JIM AND I

Jim and I were drinking
and talking about death,
which is the best way.
"When the time comes,
I hope I have the courage
to spit in his eye," I said.
"When the time comes,
I hope I have the spit,"
said Jim.

Q AND A

Did He who made the lamb make thee?
Yes, He who made the lamb made me.
But made me first, his masterstroke.
And then the lamb, his little joke.

THE DOGWOOD TREES

White is the only color
they require here.
They need not aspire
to any other in such a sea
of greens. Even then,
less than their best is quite
all right, this right-on-target off-white

POEM BEGINNING WITH A LINE
BY PHILIP LARKIN

Heaviest of flowers, the head
holds everything. Even what we believed
was long ago forgotten is still there, beyond reason,
a scent, slight, stale, but recognizable
under the thinning sweetness of decay,
season after season after season

WHERE

I tree stands where I want to stand.
The wind walks where I want to walk.
Very well.
I will stand in another place.
Very well.
I will wait for the wind to pass.

OFFICE

I went to the office.
Jim was there with a student.
He was quoting Hume.
"Sorry, you're busy.
I'll come back," I said.
"No, it's okay, sit down," Jim
said. "I'm humoring him."

ON THE WALL

On the wall in one
of the stalls in the
men's room,
someone wrote,
"I want my sweater
back." Or perhaps
it was, "I want my
sweetheart back."
It was hard to read.

ABOUT THOSE TRUE BELIEVERS

Do not be fooled because they're nice.
They are the ones who drug reason on the altar of faith,
the ones who truly practice human sacrifice.

A CLOUD

A cloud of starlings arrives out
of the blue out of the blue,
settles down in the trees
out back but briefly,
then leaves, backs out
once again the blue out of the black.

MOUNTAIN POSE

My feet are planted firmly on the earth.
But I have no feet.
My head is risen higher than the clouds.
But I have no head.
At last, I am a mountain.

TO A COLLEAGUE RECENTLY RETIRED

Tell me the truth.
So now that you have all this time
on your hands,
don't you wish, even a little bit,
that you still had all those hands on your time?

KNOWLEDGE

Knowing how paper is made,
or how ink is made,
or how a pen is made,
has nothing to do with how
a poem is made.
How lucky for the poet.

AT THE NEXT TABLE

At the next table,
a man is writing on his laptop.
He looks just like Gary Snyder.
Do not be fooled.
This means nothing at all.
For example,
I'm told I look
just like Charles Wright.

1939 PHOTOGRAPH OF MOUNT RUSHMORE

Teddy Roosevelt isn't quite done.
Scaffolding still covers his face.
He looks like Yogi Berra.
Or the umpire calling the third strike
on a disbelieving Jefferson.

MANHATTAN

I don't care what
the historians say.
I don't care what
the sociologists say.
I don't care what
the anthropologists say.
Jericho, first city,
is the gravestone of the earth.

THE DIFFERENCES

The differences
between the earth
and the world are
many, but the only
one you need to know
is the earth rotates
and the world spins.

IF THE JET

If the jet streaking across
the sky from east to west
sounds as natural to us
as the cricket in the grass,
who is to blame?

THE DAFFODILS

The daffodils
have bloomed
golden blood
so fast in the bed
by Morrison
it looks like
the morning sun
has cut its finger
climbing the fence.

BELIEF

I never believed
a black could be blacker
than the black of crows
until I saw a crow fly
through rain blacker
than the black of crows.

HOT WORK

The pileated woodpecker
with his head of fire chisels
away so hot that a mound
of tree ash has formed
around the base of the ash tree.

WORDS

"If I only had
a larger vocabulary,"
I have thought
more than once,
as though I could
do what I want
through the sheer
weight of numbers.

UPPER WEST SIDE

Why do I think the guy
washing the silver PT Cruiser
in front of his brownstone on 90th
wants me to feel like a loser?

EMILY DICKINSON IN HELL

I'm in Hell—Forever—now—
And you—are you here too?
Then there's a Billion of us!
Do tell! Hell's so—Popular—with Populace!

WILD TURKEYS

Like dirty oil
from an old
truck, the wild
turkeys leak
out of the woods
and across the road,
black drop
by black drop.

EVERY APRIL

Every April the cherry
tree puts on the same
white wedding gown
to marry the sun,
and every year
I write the same
epithalamion.

THE ARTIST'S MOTHER

The real name
of James McNeill Whistler's
painting is *Arrangement in Gray and Black No. 1.*
I've never seen No. 2.
Have you?

ADIRONDACKS

The day after
returning home
from the Adirondacks,
I could not remember
if they had been
miles of mountains
or mountains
of miles.

SO MANY GOLDFINCHES

So many goldfinches
were scattered
around the feeders
this morning,
I thought the sun
was in a head-on
collision with
last night
and shattered.

IN THE OFFICE

We were talking about Mailer.
"He was so egotistical," I said.
"No, he was so ego-testicle," said Jim.

HONEYBEES IN THE WILD CHERRY TREE

In my next life,
I want to come back
as the honeybees.
Yes, you heard me right.
Not one bee.
All of them.

GREENHOUSE

If it's so perfect in there,
why does the crimson
cyclamen pressing the glass
look like it wants to get out?

MEANS TO ENDS

Would you make
a better bed
of roses
if the only way
to do it
was to make
a sharper
crown of thorns?

CLARITY

When at last everything
becomes clear,
you will see,
for the very first time,
that it had never really
been everything.

ON THE STREET CORNER

"Even in my dream,
 I hated my hair," one said.
"So what the hell's
 the use of dreams?" said the other.

POEM BASED ON FIVE WORDS GIVEN TO MY DAUGHTER BY HER FIRST GRADE TEACHER

Like, our, play, saw, was

Like me, you are tormented by words.
Our sky is two skies.
Blackbirds play letters in them.
In yours, saw.
In mine, was.

VIEUX QUEBEC

"I can see the old city,"
my wife says.
"It doesn't look old to me,"
I say.
"Maybe they painted it,"
says my daughter.

REVIEW

He has no confidence
in verbs and nouns,
so he sends them out
surrounded by
adverbs and adjectives,
their bodyguards.

ENOUGH

Today there wasn't
enough sunlight
to fill
my coffee cup,
yet the potted paper whites
followed it
from window
to window to window.

ADAGE

Okay, okay.
One cannot make
a silk purse
from a sow's ear,
but one can
make a sow's ear
purse from
a sow's ear.

OLD HEMLOCK

The old hemlock
is the campus graybeard,
so how come no one
thought to put a bench under it?

EXACTLY

It is neither
too late
nor too early
but exactly
the right time
to be either
too late
or too early.

SO FAR

So far humans
have not
come so far.
Not really.
Not according
to the science
of such things,
the science
so far.

THE GRAND CANYON

What a joke
the gods
must have told
to cause
the earth to laugh
so hard
it split its
side laughing.

CRITICS

Last night,
through the open
window,
I heard an owl
hissing.
Funny,
I didn't think
my dream
was all
that bad.

WATCHING

The more
I watch
the birds
from my window,
the more
I am convinced
that the wrong people
are people.

EMILY DICKINSON'S BEDROOM

Neat as a pin,
just like the poems
that prick the skin
and, drop by drop,
bleed us from within.

OLD CHINESE SAYING

Calling things by
their right names
is the first step on
the journey to wisdom.
Okay.
Now what?

SOME THINGS

Some things are
just so crazy
to think about
that we
have no choice
except to
do them
without thinking.

SWAMP

The half-submerged
log where yesterday
four turtles sunbathed
today has nothing
but a space
the size of four turtles.

ART

John Coltrane
practiced so many
hours a day,
the reeds
of his saxophone
turned red.

BEGONIA

Little red-headed stoic,
the begonia
keeps taking
the raindrops' beating
all morning,
even without
shoulders,
shrugging it off.

SHORT SPEECH FOR CAIN

The kid
sacrificed a kid.
I wanted
to go one better,
so I sacrificed him
on my altar.

THE DREAM

In the dream
I was invisible
until I passed
through the world
of invisible mirrors
and saw myself.

THE DIFFERENCE

Prose is a 40-watt bulb.
Enough to read by.
Poetry is a 4000-watt floodlight.
Enough to blind you.

RELATIVITY

In the good dream,
I begged for my living.
In the bad dream,
I begged for my life.

AN ANSWER

When the rabbi in his sermon
said, "It is a sin
to desire completion,"
I left my religion.

ON BEING TOLD MY POEMS SEEM FORCED

You know, you're right.
They do indeed seem forced.
But there is a simple explanation.
My poems are my children.

READING FROST'S "THE GUM-GATHERER"

Robert sure had balls.
This gum-gatherer is none other
than Wordsworth's leech-gatherer
in flannel shirt and overalls.

THISTLE DOWN

Before drifting
at the mercy
of the wind,
it is freed
by the justice
of the wind.

DIALOGUE

"No time like the present,"
said the surgeon.
"No present like the time,"
agreed the patient.

CINQUAIN

Crocus.
Spring morning walk.
The lake ice nearly gone.
Suddenly a black shadow's wings:
Crow curse.

SIGN OF SPRING

The stop sign
in the parking lot
is a single red rose
in a gray garden.

APHORISMS

Sometimes
sayings
have to
be said
out of
the need
to put
some
times
into words.

CONCERT

The oratorio ended.
My daughter said,
"You have a bass clap, dad."

DECEMBER MORNING

The snow
has turned
the world old
overnight.
Therefore,
I will not
ask anything
of it today.

SEX

These days,
I'd be satisfied
with just
going through
the motions
of going
through
the motions.

THE TURN

I get to the corner.
I turn right and
cut the future
in half.

NEIGHBOR

So many children
running around
in the yard,
we knew
he must
have been dying

WHEN THE ADMINISTRATOR

When the administrator
finally finished his
inarticulate speech,
Jim blurted out,
"My sentiments
approximately!"

POEM

Some things
need to be words,
and some
things need
to be
themselves,
including
words.

THE MORNING FREIGHT

Did you see it?
No?
How well
it covers
its tracks.

EARLY JANUARY

The geese
are crying
in the distance.
Or is that the distance
crying in
the geese?

CONFESSION

I am
faithful
to my
wife.
And that's
the long
and
the short
of it.

THE TRUTH

So hypnotic,
I can't take
my eyes
off of it.
The pot is boiling.

BIRTHDAY

I approach my
seventieth year,
slowly, carefully,
from behind,
so as not to
frighten it away.

QUESTION FOR THE ORACLE

Know thyself.
Okay.
Nothing in excess.
Okay.
But does that
include
knowing
thyself?

SPRING

My neighbor
removes
the cover from
his red Vette.
Ah!
First flower
of spring!

DEFENSE

How do you expect
me to eat crow
with my foot
in my mouth?

OF WEI QINGZHI

Of Wei Qingzhi
almost nothing
is known. He
planted 1000
chrysanthemums.
But that alone
is everything.

TIME

It is neither
yours
to give
nor mine
to receive,
yet
so warm
from our hands.

FROM THE WINDOW

The rain off
the duck's back
was like water off
a duck's back.

TO TAKE

To take too much
for granted
first requires
too much
be left
for granted.

ISSA

It means cup of tea,
which, for most,
he is not.
Oh, unfortunately.

POEM AT 5:01 A.M.

Most deaths
of natural causes
occur, scientists
say, between
3 and 5 am.

RICHARD EBERHART DEAD AT 101

Happily for us,
of poets it cannot be said
we outlive our usefulness.

OCTOBER

It is April's opposite.
With new buds of death,
the trees flower yellow, orange, red.

NEWS OF THE PASSING
OF GRANDMOTHER KARP AT 98

The doctor said heart failure.
We know better.
It was heart success.
Congratulations, Granny!

IN POETRY

In poetry
there are no
wrong words.
There are only
sour notes.

THE SKY

Th sky without
a cloud is like
the mind without
an idea.

APOLOGY

What I had
in mind
is not
what I
had in
mind.

EPITAPH FOR A BOXER

I couldn't
beat him
to death,
so I beat
him to death.

SIMILE

The good memory
sits heavily
on your mind
like a bad memory.

SHIT HAIKU

Again the toilet.
Many delicious dried plums.
But this haiku is shit.

ANOTHER OLD CHINESE SAYING

What good are
one-thousand bows
if there is only
one arrow?

AGNOSTICISM

I can be convinced,
but it will have to
be in person.

DEPARTURE

It left
before my
very eyes
right before
my very
eyes.

A PHOTO OF ME

Shit, how I envy
all the millions
who died before
photography.

POEM AT 7:30 AM

What can
be more
beautiful than
a red
frying pan?

NEWS ITEM

VIRGIN AIRLINES SELLS $250,000 TICKETS FOR
FIVE-MINUTE SPACE FLIGHT

Now there's
a vacation
worth its
weightlessness
in gold.

MENTAL NOTE TO MY WIFE

No post-mortem
for the post fallen, please.
Bring it up next time.

MARCH 14

Today is
Einstein's birthday.
The sun
is shining.

THE LAST PARADOX

When it's time
to go,
there's no time
to go.

SHE SAID HE SAID

She:
I remembered everything.
He:
I remembered you remembering everything.

PEACE

Peace of body
is always
required for
peace of mind.

LAYING BLAME

They didn't
make love
anymore
because she
couldn't
stand him.

LAST REQUEST

I want to die
like there's
no tomorrow.

GOD GIVES HOPE

Road Sign for the Calvary Assembly Church

Hope we
have already.
Who's giving
the certainty?

HELL

Hell is heaven's parody.
Unless it's the other
way around.

AT THE GYM

Working out
is not
working out.

EDUCATION

Some things
cannot be learned.
Learning,
for instance.

POSITIONAL

I'm under
no illusions.
I'm over
them.

POST-COITAL

It all
comes
down to
this.

TIME

One
irreplaceable
moment
after
another.

EXCUSES

I'm a poet.
What's yours?

HAMLET

Revenge play
with
a vengeance.

NOWHERE

The original word
for here.

PESSIMISM

Time
after
time
after
time.

OPTIMISM

Time
before
time
before
time.

NO NEWS

Good news
all day today.

GOOD NEWS

No news
all day today.

THE PHILOSOPHY OF APPLE

il
ithink
itherefore
il
iam.

VERY SHORT SPEECH FOR A NEW HUSBAND

Look, ma,
no hands.

THE SECRET

It goes
without
saying.

POLITICS

All poetry
is local.

THE PASSING OF A NOTED CRITIC

Detraction
was
the attraction.

THE SUREST WAY TO FOOL YOURSELF
INTO BELIEVING ANYTHING YOU WANT

Make up
your mind.

VERY SHORT SPEECH FOR LAZARUS

Jesus,
what
a dream.

NEWSPAPER

Today's suicide note.

IN THE TERMINAL

Interminable.

from **THE BLACK BIRCH** (2017)

ROSE BUSHES IN EARLY MARCH

All winter the thorns were their flowers.
They had them to themselves.
Soon they will wish they could turn around
on their stems, twist themselves to face
inward instead of out,
welcoming the roses back.

UNDER A BLUE SPRUCE

Under a blue spruce,
a little pink thing
trying its hardest
to be a flower
has just been
rewarded with a bee.

MORNING IN LATE NOVEMBER

The blast from the shotgun
startles the wood duck from the water.
What shall I do with my anger,
which is louder than the wood duck's cry
but not as loud as the shotgun?

THE ONLY DEFINITION OF POETRY
YOU'LL EVER NEED

"Poetry," said the poet from Brooklyn,
"is that sort of writing you can read
silently to yourself on the train
or the bus and not be embarrassed
by moving your lips."

THE ONLY SWAN POEM YOU'LL EVER NEED

Swans feed in the estuary.
Their long, white, graceful
necks are dirty.

THE ONLY ZEN POEM YOU'LL EVER NEED

Think
nothing
of it.

THE ONLY EROTIC POEM YOU'LL EVER NEED

Eros
backwards
is
sore.

THE ONLY TRUE STORY ABOUT HEAVEN
AND HELL YOU'LL EVER NEED

"What do you do in heaven?"
 the pastor asked the little boy.
"You sit on a cloud and play the harp."
"And what do you do in hell?"
 he asked the little boy.
"You sit on fire and play the accordion."

THE WORLD

"The world is going to hell
 in a hand basket," I said to Jim.
"Impossible," Jim said. "Why?"
 I asked. "Because the hand basket
 would burn up long before
 it got there," said Jim down the hall.

WHEN THE TIME COMES

 We were in the office.
 We were talking about death.
"When the time comes, Jim," I said,
"I hope I'm gonna spit in death's eye."
"When the time comes, Joel," Jim said,
"I hope I have spit."

THE WORDS

Let us live here,
we who have
no place else to go.

from **I, EMILY DICKINSON & OTHER FOUND POEMS** (2018)

THE NEWS

(From a student essay, date unknown)

Television news
annoys me
because
it invades
people's privates.

A NICE PLACE TO VISIT

(conversation between a mother and daughter
overheard at the Hayden Planetarium, date unknown)

"Mommy, the universe
 is such a big scary place."
"Oh, yes, it is a big scary place,
 but don't worry, dear, we're not going there."

CLASSIFIED

(from an 1860 advertisement for Pony Express riders)

Wanted:
Young, skinny,
wiry fellows
not over 18,
must be expert riders,
willing to risk
death daily.
Orphans preferred.

BUDDHIST BULLSEYE

(from a sign in the Junior Department of Target)

The look of
the moment.
Infinity scarves.

KOAN

(from a story by Bruno Schulz)

Unlit
lightning.

I STAND CORRECTED

(from a college lecture overheard in the hallway, date unknown)

We anthropologists
have to be as gender
neutral in our language
as possible. That's why
I say critters a lot.

VOICE OF THE MOURNING DOVE

(from *A Field Guide to the Birds* by Roger Tory Peterson, 1947)

A hollow mournful,
Ooah, cooo, cooo, cooo.
At a distance,
Only the three cooos are audible.

BAD FORTUNE

(from *The New York Times*, date unknown)

Donald Lau
spent a decade
writing fortunes
for the biggest
chinese fortune
cookie maker
until he suffered
from writer's block
and had to retire.

WORDS OF WISDOM

(from a Sumerian clay tablet circa 3,000 B.C.E.,
National Geographic, date unknown)

We are all
doomed to die.
Let us spend.

HIGHER LEARNING

(from a student essay, date unknown)

Since I've been
in college,
I've learned
servile things.

FOR YOUR REFERENCE

(from the titles of vocabulary books
in Barnes & Noble)

Word power made easy
1200 essential words you should know to sound smart
1100 words you need to know
504 absolutely essential words
101 misused words
100 words every high school graduate should know

from *IN SHORT ORDER* (2018)

AUGUST AFTERNOON

The clouds are so white,
so bright, so lit
with the sun's reflection,
so light,
there is nothing cloudy about them.

A FARM

A farm without
a silo is like, oh,
I don't know,
like a woman
without a man?

TWILIGHT

At twilight the light
is the shadow of the light
while the shadows
are the light of the shadows.

THE LEAVES

The leaves are dead
before they fall,
the best way to die,
denying gravity
the satisfaction
of the ground.

A NOISE

I thought it was
a helicopter, but
it was only an angel,
his wings breaking
off, cursing as he fell.

AT THE END OF SUMMER

At the end of summer,
the summer's sounds
sign off sounding off,
soundly convincing now
after a whole summer
simply sounding them out.

AT THE CORNER

At the corner of
the concrete slab
of the garden shed,
what no weed wanted,
a clover cult has
established itself.

ANY POEM BY JOHN ASHBERY

Where poetry
goes when it
wants to be
alone.

FEEDBACK

"So do the finches
like the new feeder?"
my wife asks me.
"Look out the window,"
I answer. "They're
all back to feed."

FROM THE CAFÉ KITCHEN

From the cafe kitchen
come the cooking sounds,
come the cooking smells,
but if the food is bad or good
it is impossible to tell.

FULFILLMENT CENTER

The book I ordered
from Amazon arrived
today from the fulfillment
center and has become,
for now, the center
of my fulfillment.

GUGGENHEIM

The Calder mobile
under the rotunda
is immobile.

IT RAINED JUST ENOUGH

It rained just enough
to turn the tops
of the lily pads
from green to silver
but not a drop more.

OCTOBER

The trees, part
red, part yellow,
part orange, have
feet in two seasons,
but the evergreens,
ever green, stand apart.

KAFKA

Kafka said the most
momentous events
in a person's life occur
at 9 am. Yesterday at
9 am I took a crap. Today
at 9 am I shaved. Tomorrow
at 9 am I'll be teaching
the comma. Damn.
He was right.

MY GARDEN

Tend your garden, Voltaire said.
But I was a teenager in the Bronx
when I read *Candide*, and we
didn't have a garden. I didn't know
what to do, so I just tended to my
own business by staying off the streets
after dark.

THE AIR

The air is so still,
the thistledown
have nowhere
to go but down.

ON A BEE

The best poem
ever written on a bee
is by Emily Dickinson,
so why are you wasting
your time reading this one?

SUNDAY

This morning the music
coming from the United
Congregationalist Church
was so loud, the organist
must have pulled out
all the stops.

THE CROWS

The crows in the treetops
are lords of morning.
Only the lone C-130
leaving town for
Afghanistan raises
more heads.

THE GEESE

The geese on
the lake do not
care how shallow
the bottom is
but only how
deep the top is.

THE MOTORCYCLE

The motorcycle roars down
the street like the wild animal the rider,
dressed entirely in the skin
of a cow, has always wanted to be.

THE SQUEAKY WHEEL

The insects in the trees
make the sound
of machinery mellowed
mild by the sun's golden oil.

THE WAVES

The waves of thunder
overhead do not stop
the birds from singing out
from under the tree cover.

THE WOMAN

The woman with the long legs
and no bra in the café
reading Kafka aroused
my curiosity.

TO MY ARTHRITIS

I'll see you in hell, Art.
In the meantime,
I hope you appreciate
your home away from home.

WE WERE TALKING

We were talking about the worst
thing that could happen to us.
Losing our sight we agreed.
"I'd get a gun and put
a bullet in my head," I said.
"What a waste," Jim said.
"I'd do a good deed and marry
an ugly woman to take care of me."

WINNERS AND LOSERS

Of course, they are everywhere,
for that is all there are anywhere.
Nature, it seems, has no use for
compromise but has good use
for the compromised. Just
follow the flies.

THE WEEPING WILLOW

The weeping willow at
the swamp weeps
because its companion
sycamore has drowned.

MOVIES

Leaving the movie,
the music still in my ears,
I looked up to see a sky
so celestially perfect,
so celestial, I could swear
I was in another movie.

THE AFTERNOON TRAIN

The afternoon train,
a splinter of silver on
the other side of the river
heading south out of Ossining,
was a miniature river.

REQUEST

Leave me alone,
but don't
leave me
alone.

FOR THEODORE ROETHKE WHO SAID THAT EVERY LINE OF A POEM SHOULD BE A POEM

How am I doing so far?

AS I SIT IN THE SUN

As I sit in the sun,
reading, a butterfly,
a little white one,
alights on my arm,
grooms itself for a
moment, then flies off.
I put down the book
and close my eyes.
"No, James Wright,
I have not wasted my
life. Life has wasted me."

A HOLE IN MY SHIRT

There is a hole in my shirt.
It is a small hole.
It is the size of my little finger.
It is just over my heart.
That is good.
If there has to be a hole in my shirt,
I would not want it in any other place.

BROTHER WREN

Brother Wren, when I hear you sing,
I wish I were you, so I could mind
my own business without questioning
what my business is, or what my mind is,
which are the same. Every little thing
without questioning is the purest way to sing.

GREEN

There's so much green,
one cannot help but wonder
what the earth is envying.
The rusty red rocks of Mars?
The moon and its silvery sheen?
Or simply the way its own wan winter was.

ON EDGE

I was on edge
all day, but even so,
even after many tries,
I still could not get a word
in edgewise.

HOW TO SIT

Always make sure
there's an empty chair
next to yours for the one
who has nothing on his mind,
so you can learn how he
attained enlightenment.

MAY AFTERNOON

Green and blue and white
are the three colors of the world.
Such vivid green, such vivid blue,
such vivid white, they are out of this world.
Such bright green, such bright blue, such
bright white, they are out of sight.

PLOP!

In the shallow inlet of the lake,
a small pond's size, the very big snapper,
at my approach, lets herself in with a plop!
much louder than any old frog's.

THE VARNISHED TRUTH

Are you worried?
Are you worried about the future?
Are you worried about poetry?
So many variables.
So much future.
So much poetry.
So much to vanish right before your eyes.

TO MEAN NOTHING MEANS A LOT

A bumblebee stumbles
sidelong in broken circles
about the underside
of the blue umbrella outside
making it appear it flies
beneath two skies.

LOST AND FOUND

It's usually the other way around, isn't it?
Found and lost?
Or did I misunderstand?
Is it "found out" and "lost out"
that I was thinking about?

SPILLWAY

As I get nearer
to the spillway,
the sound of the
falling water rises.

NEW ENGLAND

So what is there about Massachusetts,
New Hampshire, Vermont, etc. anyway
that makes poets want to live there?
Is it fucking Puritans?
No. It must be something else.
No. It is. It's fucking Puritans.

AMERICA

Singing?
Are you kidding?
I hear America rapping.
I haven't heard America singing since 1968.

THE LAST PATCH OF SNOW

The last patch of snow,
snatched by the sun
from the shadow of an oak,
wants to go quietly,
softly weeping to itself,
but the tree frogs,
with other ideas, sing
a march tune, so happily, so raucously.

AT THE DENTIST

In the dentist's waiting room,
I asked one of two little boys
who were waiting for their father,
"Are you twins?" "Yes," he said,
and then I asked the other,
"Are you twins?" "No," he said.
Neither one laughed.

THOUGHT

In terms of thought,
here I am,
on thought's terms.

CEASE AND DESIST

What I want to know
is how to desist
without ceasing.

DAVID

David is not David.
David is Goliath.
We are David.
He is not concerned with us.
He does not even know we exist.
He is intent on his sheep, big as elephants, as they
graze on grass up to our necks.

THE LADY PHYSICIST'S NAME FOR
THE ORIGIN OF THE UNIVERSE

The Bigger Banger

THE ONLY MEMORABLE LINE OF A POEM
I'VE FORGOTTEN

The rose's politics is the daisy's war.

WEATHERVANE

Whether vain or not,
don't we all follow
the winds of our folly?
Aren't we all tin cutouts
of roosters, of pigs, of whales,
of little men in little row boats fishing?

BIRDBATH

The Mexican birdbath is
so colorful, so vibrantly beautiful,
the birds do not come to it.
I do not blame them.
I wouldn't either if the three
hand-painted ceramic poets perched
on the rim were more colorful,
more vibrantly beautiful than I.

VIVA!

Lorca. Sabines. Mistral. Neruda. Viva!
Pinera. Vallejos. Marti. de la Vega. Viva!
Mendoza. Uribe. Paz. de la Silva. Viva!
de Gongora. Cardenal. Dario. Zamora. Viva!
Herrera. Cisneros. Machado. Rivera. Viva!

DUET

On the piano bench,
mother primo, daughter secundo,
as though mother is playing
with herself at her daughter's age,
daughter's wrong notes
cannot explain mother's smile.

O, GENERAL

The rockets.
The bombs.
The woman buried alive.
The child burned but alive.
"A war to the death," the general says.
O, general, what war is not a war to the death?
O, general, logic plus logic equals insanity.
O, general, the world is the saddest place on earth.

ONE WORD

One word
leads to
another, and
someday
perhaps I'll
discover
exactly what
that word is.

from *TOMORROW, TODAY, AND YESTERDAY* (2019)

CALIBAN

They are gone, all gone.
And Ariel, too. Good riddance.
The place is mine, all mine!
Oh shit . . . There's no one left to curse.

SHORT SPEECH FOR SISYPHUS

See how I torment
my tormentor by
cutting him out.
See how I punish
myself by pushing
this stone I cut up
this mountain I built.

TOY POEM

This is my toy poem.
I hope you like it.
I made it in the workshop.
I sawed it and sanded it
and glued it and screwed
it and painted it and
finished it to a glossy
finish and signed my name
on the bottom of it.
Please don't pick it up.
Please don't play with it.
It will fall apart.

IF TREES COULD WEEP

If pine and oak, ash
and larch, sassafras
and sycamore, if all
could weep, they should
weep like the weeping
cherry weeps whose snow
white tears are more
beautiful than laughter.

WHEN EMILY

When Emily came into the house
and the door didn't close
completely behind her,
she called out, "Dad, could
you close the rest of the door?"

QUESTION FOR YAHWEH

If, as it is said, you are omnipotent,
and since, as it is said, that means
for you all things are possible, why
the hell are you always so old?

SOMEDAY

Someday the last poet in the world
will write the last poem,
and someday the last reader
in the world will read it and
say to herself, "Where is Emily
Dickinson when you need her?"

TIMELINE

In 1819 Walt Whitman is born.
In 1821 John Keats dies.
In 1883 William Carlos Williams is born.
In 1892 Walt Whitman dies.
Think about this for a moment.

IMPATIENCE

How impatient life is.
The ice is not yet gone
from the lake, and the carp
are already awake with both
eyes, and as I watched,
two mourning doves mated.

WILLOW

Willow may be old,
but it hasn't forgotten
how to make green green.

SITTING ON A BENCH

Sitting on a bench in the park
trying to think of nothing,
I sneezed. A stranger passing
by said, "Bless you." I said, "Thank
you." I must have succeeded
in thinking of nothing, for
I really felt blessed, and I really
was thankful.

NOW THAT

Now that the cherry tree
in front of the house looks
like every other tree, I will
look at every other tree
with my cherry tree eyes.

IMPROVISATION

When my wife
is out of sorts,
the solution
is at hand.

RECREATION

We, too, are here in summer
at the seashore, playing
to make ourselves again for
the workings of another year.

POETRY MONTH AT STORM KING

Everything was fine
at Kay Ryan's reading
until someone in the toilet
nearby, the door open,
flushed down her last line.

THE MOON OVER THE HILL
IN THE MIDDLE OF THE DAY

O, over-the-hill
movie star,
so that's what
you look like
without all
the face powder.

CEMETERY UNDER THREE FEET OF SNOW

Only the tops of the tallest
stones are visible. The rest
are buried totally, as buried
as those buried beneath them.
I do not linger. Instead, I will
return in spring, when the snow
is gone and all the stones are
open in the sun like gray flowers
among the daffodils. When death
really hits home.

DETOUR

How lost we are
off the beaten track.
When we have to go
back, how taken aback.

THE SKYLIGHT OF THE WESTCHESTER MALL

If everything that is precious
to us can be found only in glass
cases, then for whom are we precious
in this glass case we find ourselves?
And for whom is that perfect blue
and white heaven heaven?

SWANS

While the five swans swim,
many geese wait on the shore.
The swans swim.
And swim.

FALLEN BARN

Like a house of cards,
the barn of cards
could not stand up under
one more ace of years.

BAD DAY AT THE PIANO

Today you forgot
Chopin's address.
I heard your fingers
running around
the white avenues
and the black
streets looking
for his house.

CLAIM TO FAME

At the Linden Tree Inn
in Rockport, Massachusetts,
I sat on the same toilet seat
that Judy Collins sat on.

PRESENT

"What do you want for your
  birthday?" she asked.
"Let's just get something
  straight," he answered.

DIALOGUE

"You're so predictable.
  You're a cartoon," she said.
"What can I say? I'm out
  of my depth," he answered.

ALMOST DOESN'T COUNT

The rain is so cold
it's almost ice
while the ice is so
warm it's almost rain.

TYPO

How you laughed when you read
what the editor of that magazine
had done to your poem, changing,
in the last line, "salvia," as though
it had been you who had made
the error, to "saliva."

UTILITY

The utility pole
on the road at
the bottom of
the driveway
was once a tree
without utility.

THE END

The poems stop not because
the poet loses his voice.
The poems stop because
the poet goes deaf.

SONG

I have always wanted
(at least ever since
reading Creeley) to write
a poem called "Song."
Hey nonny nonny.

from *IF YOU SHOULD SEE ME WALKING ON THE ROAD* (2019)

AN OLD MIRROR

Here is one for the old,
this antique mirror that
has gone blind from
lifetimes of staring into
the light. This is the one
to take them into its soft
glass arms, to keep them,
and sing them to sleep,
the old.

TO MY DESK CHAIR

Thank you
for putting me
in my place.

MEETING

When the Chair told us not
to worry about the new policy
because the VP for Academic
Affairs said it wasn't cast in
concrete but was "written in sand,"
Jim blurted out, "Yeah but sand
is an ingredient of concrete."

APRIL

Now I lack
for nothing,
for I lie here in
the sun, inhaling
the lilac.

REPUTATION

Galway Kinnell's
"Holy Shit" is
the kind of poem
that gives poetry
a bad name.

A PORTRAIT OF THE ARTIST

He looks as if
he is gazing out
a window or walking
through a door.
Mind you, this is
all the time.

POETS

Nietzsche had it wrong when
he said, "I don't like poets:
They lie." Didn't he realize that's
the only reason one should like
poets, the way they charm your
socks off while lying to your face?

ON THE SURFACE

Cut through the world,
and you reveal the surfaces
of the inner world. Cut through
that, and you reveal more surfaces.
As long as we have eyes to see,
there are surfaces to be seen.
This is why blindness is so closely
associated with wisdom.

LAW & ORDER

The only way
to stop a bad
poet with a pen
is a good poet
with a gun.

from *TRUE ENOUGH* (2019)

WHEN THE HONEYBEE

When the honeybee flew
from the flowering shrub
it had been gathering pollen
on, I swear I could see a smile
on the face of the flowering
shrub in the place where a face
would be if it had one.

HELGA

She should never
have agreed
to appear in that
film about him,
that fat old woman
in that ridiculous hat.
At least he was
dead by then.

MY NEIGHBOR

I don't believe a body has a soul,
but I do believe a soul has a body.
I saw the body on the floor where
he left it. I heard the soul crying
from the cat on the bed where
he left it.

SEPHORA

Did Moses' Midianite wife,
Zipporah, really use all this
perfume, all this lipstick, all
this eye shadow, all this eye liner,
all this lash lengthener, all this
body lotion, that if I weren't
already seventy-seven and thereby
have no reason to, I'd swear off sex?

THE DARK CLOUDS

The dark clouds so flow
over the sky to overflowing
that when I heard the siren
of the fire truck heading east,
I thought it was responding
to tomorrow burning.

THE BIRD

The bird in the beech tree
can count to two—
Whit who—
and three—
Whit who whee—
but not to one
apparently.

THE DIFFERENCE

The day is
the night
with light
but with
less on
its mind.

THE PURPLE CHRYSANTHEMUM

The purple chrysanthemum
is halfway dead, its brown
dead half imparting its living
purple half with a desperate
liveliness wholly its own.

THE LAKE IN THE RAIN

The lake in the rain
remembers when it was
the rain and quietly cries
in the depths of its sleep,
which, if you carefully
listen, sounds like rain
on a lake.

THE THREE-MONTH OLD

The three-month old in
the stroller was staring
at me. What was she thinking?
I tell you honestly, I would pay
her college tuition to know
what was in her three-month
old mind while staring me.

WITH NOT A CLOUD ALL DAY

With not a cloud all day
to contest it, the sun had
the sky to itself until a crow
looked, then came to cast
the scowl of itself across the blue.

EXCUSE

I wanted to tell the truth,
but you see, the truth had
better things to do and
wouldn't let me.

JIM AND I WENT TO VISIT

Jim and I went to visit a colleague
in the nursing home. "He's in good
spirits," I said. "Yeah, but I would
rather the good spirits be in me,"
said Jim.

KOOSER

Ted, you say your poem
about your dead parents
is dark. I say you do darkness
with a light touch so the
rest of us may see better in it.

from *FOR ALL I KNOW* (2020)

THE PAINTING MI FU BOWING
TO ELDER BROTHER STONE BY YU MING

Mi Fu by bowing
has made a rock
of himself.
Elder Brother Stone
by being bowed
to does not change.
The space between
them, however, changes.

AFTER A CHINESE POEM

Not eager for news, I am the recluse
who will not answer the door for fear
he will open to one who comes this near
only to ask the way to another's house.

NATURE AND SUPERNATURE

To fly fleet enough from the natural
to arrive at the supernatural
means miracle's means.

SHORT SPEECH FOR ADAM

When I woke up from
that deep sleep,
I saw her there,
standing a few yards
away, in the shade
of two trees, with
her hands on her hips,
speaking to me
in the language
of the hyenas.

WALKING BY THE MARSH

I disturbed a hawk
but saved a field mouse
it had its on eye on.
How we take sides
without thinking.

THE BIG BROWN

The big brown leaf tumbled
so slowly down,
so deliberately turned
while downward
over, I thought it was
a wren showing off.

THE DAY BEFORE

The day before
the swamp freezes
over, the black water
seizes the sun
and pulls it under.

CLOUDS

They look the same
from up here above them
except there are more
of them, and they have
less to say.

THE WASATCH

On the trail, lightning
and thunder followed us.
The gods were angry,
but not with me, for that
is not my sort of flattery.

BRIDAL VEIL FALLS

It is named for
an Indian legend.
Ah, the best kind.

TWO OLD INDIANS

"They sound like chattering
crows, don't they?" one said.
"Yeah, but I understand crows.
I don't understand that tribe,"
the other said.

THE PASSENGER JET

The passenger jet leaves
its long, broken contrail
straight across the sky behind
as if it were the dotted line of
the contract the skywriter must sign.

from **ENJOY YOURSELF** (2020)

HOME

We are so adaptable,
so amazingly adaptable,
that no matter where
we find ourselves,
we manage to make
ourselves at home,
even at home,
even there.

A SMALL CLOUD

A small cloud drifts overhead.
The cloud is actually eight small clouds.
It is an island chain of clouds.
Soon it evaporates.
Soon it disappears.
I must remember this when I am asked,
"What is the soul?"

SUDDENLY

Suddenly, a hundred
black birds cracked out
of the trees into the open
as though a long shadow long
in the shadows was free to go.

BARELY

Barely visible
in the blue,
the moon, like
a slender bit
of white cloud,
is just enough up
there to keep up
keeping it up.

THE BARE MAXIMUM

At most, it is
the least
you can do.

THE DIFFERENCE

The difference between
rock and stone is not
geology. It is how much
you can carry in one hand.

THE BLACK HOLE

The black hole at
the center of poetry
wants to suck all
the words down into it.
Fortunately, the Chinese
invented paper.

I WISH

I wish God existed so
I could hear him ask
for forgiveness.
I cannot think of any other
reason to wish God existed.

IN THE HYDRANGEA

In the hydrangea,
one savage butterfly
salvages what's left
of summer.

LET'S PLAY THE SIN LIKE THE VIOLIN

Let's play the sin like the violin.
Let it begin in the dark and end in the stratosphere.
Let only the angels hear.
Let's take it on the chin.
They will lose.
We will win.
Let only the angels stare.

THE LAW OF ATTRACTION

It is said that all
the magnetic force
in the universe is not
equal to the force of
one magnet on the door
of your refrigerator, so
is this why I am more
attracted to my beer
than to the universe?

FALSE MODESTY

I would rather have
a hundred false starts
than one false ending.

SINGLE FILES

In the same single file
as the deer family,
a trail of deer shit
incrementally leads me
across the lawn excrementally.

PROXIMITY

The orchard is next
to the cemetery.
This must be why
the honey crisp taste
so good. The crispy,
sweet dead.

WHEN THE DARK

When the dark rain clouds
moved over, broad banks of
bright clouds were left above
the rain clouds' altitude
to change the whole day's
attitude left behind.

TELL ME AGAIN

Tell me again
what I was told
when I was young
what poetry is
supposed to do.
I am old.
I am old.
I have forgotten.

RHETORICAL ANSWER

All things
end up
winding
down.

from **THE TIME OF YOUR LIFE** (2020)

OUTSIDE

The rain stops,
the sun comes out,
and for the first time in my life,
I have gotten a hard-on for a fucking flower.

PURPLE

Everyone looks good in it.
Everything looks wonderful in it.
The sky looks good in purple.
The purple marten looks wonderful in it.
The emperors and empresses,
regardless of their cruelty,
looked good, looked wonderful in purple.

MASTURBATION

Sorry,
my mistake,
I got ahead
of myself.

METAMORPHOSIS

Does the monarch butterfly
on the viburnum
know it was not always a butterfly,
or is it only where memory
ends that wings begin?

ON THE PASSING OF PHILIP ROTH

Philip Roth
is dead.
Just feel
this cloth.

REASSURANCE

"Nothing's humming today," I said.
"Hey, don't complain," said Jim.
"Humming is what you do
  when you've forgotten the words."

THE NOWHERE

The nowhere
to be found
is not the same
nowhere
as the nowhere
to be seen.

from **THE MOON IS THE CAPITAL OF THE WORLD** (2020)

CLEMATIS

Such a friendly flower,
the clematis drapes its long, purple arm over
the shoulder of the deer fence.

BELIEF

When the bee that found
the hundred evening primrose
flowers returns, who in the hive
will ever believe its fantastical
tale of El Dorado?

READING

As I crossed
the stage to
the lectern,
I was worried
as to how my
poems would
come across.

JULIE

Her pair of scissors
is the key to my lock
of hair, so now I shall
never go elsewhere.

POOR PHOEBE

She keeps one
eye on her nest
and one on me.

AUBADE

At the crack of dawn,
the neighbor down
the road who leaves for work
on his Harley-Davidson
gives new meaning to
the crack of dawn.

MY MUSE AND HER HUSBAND, JIM BEAM

They make such a lovely
couple, Euterpe and he.
How happy in the extreme,
Mr. and Mrs. Jim Beam.

ROOF

The roof is the blessing of the house.
The roof keeps its hands on the walls.
Only the roof knows the sky and what comes from
        the sky.
The roof knows the birds by heart.
The roof knows the clouds inside out.
Because no one visits it, the roof is the loneliest part
        of the house.
Because no one bothers it, the roof is the wisest
        part of the house.

A POEM FOR THE MOUNTAIN

A poem for the mountain
is not the same as a poem
for the valley. Nevertheless,
you cannot write a poem for
the valley without mentioning
at least two mountains.

THERE WAS A WHITE STALLION WITH RED EARS

It had a French name.
I rode on his back across the heat wave.
I rowed the doldrums.
I sang a rowing song into his red ear.
Fog appeared.
A rock appeared in the fog.
A hard place appeared in the haze.
I cursed them in the French language.
An albino buffalo trampled my idea of history to death.

THE SUN THAT SETS

The sun that sets in the west
in the west is not the same sun
that sets in the west in the east.
To this I can attest.

from *A GUIDE OF THE PERPLEXED* (2020)

IT WAS QUIET

The only voice was the crow's.
It was speaking from the heart.
"Listen, I'm speaking from the heart," it said.
"But don't you always speak from the heart?" I said.
"Yes, I do. But you do not always listen from the heart,"
it said.
It flew off.
It was quiet again.
It was twice as quiet.

SONG

The woodpecker
in the tree behind
me is not singing
the woodpecker's
song. It is singing
the song of the tree.

THERE IS JUST ENOUGH SUN

There is just enough sun
angling late in to show
the wild cherry's shadow
on the house's side like
a black and white movie
shown in slow motion
slowed to the slowest
motion that can be shown.

AFTER THE READING

After the reading, he said
he didn't know the first thing
about it, which is very bad
because one thing is all
there ever is to know about it.

MY JAPANESE DEATH POEM

When I die, bury
me with an acorn
in my mouth so
one of us at least
might become the
mighty oak tree both
our mothers wanted.

I WALK THE RAILROAD TRACKS

with you as my mind's companion,
Galway Kinnell, your fellow Euclidean.
The tracks are straight here and point
straight to where they vanish through
the trees. You were eighty-seven.
I am seventy-eight. The prostrate is
enlarged, the arthritis tightening. I'm
on the way, all right. Now, for the
first time, I see it. I see the point in
vanishing completely out of sight.

AFTER THE DOWNPOUR

After the downpour,
the sun pours down
unabated all day,
playing the geese on
the lake with its silver
line and its golden hook.

THERE IS A HOLE IN YOUR LIFE

It is a peephole.
It is big enough for one eye only.
It is for a peep show for one eye only.

BEHIND

What now is
just right behind
will almost always
eventually be just
left behind.

THE MOST BEAUTIFUL POEM
IN THE ENGLISH LANGUAGE

According to William R. Espy's *Book of Lists*, the
ten most beautiful English words are gonorrhea,
gossamer, lullaby, meandering, mellifluous,
murmuring, onomatopoeia, Shenandoah, summer
afternoon, and wisteria.

On a summer afternoon,
meandering along the Shenandoah,
smelling the wisteria,
murmuring a mellifluous onomatopoeia
lullaby to a beautiful lady in gossamer,
I contracted gonorrhea.

WHY THERE'S NO MONUMENT
IN WASHINGTON D.C. TO JOHN ADAMS

"Because," said my colleague
in the history department,
"he was a complete and utter asshole."

THE MISTAKE THE MYSTICS MAKE

It is a small mistake.
It is this.
The mystics mistake the god for the goddess.
It is an understandable mistake.
It is a case of mistaken identity.
But it doesn't take much to correct.
It takes only one dream to correct.

MOE WAS MY FAVORITE STOOGE

He was the boss.
He was the brains of the outfit.
He was a more Hitlerish Hitler than Chaplin.
He always had the best looking wife.
Or was that Larry?

DO YOU EAT THE SUN FOR BREAKFAST?

The sun is good for breakfast.
Do you eat the clouds for lunch?
The clouds are good for lunch.
Do you eat the moon for dinner?
The moon is bad for dinner.
The moon will give you indigestion.
The moon will give you bad dreams.

from *PIANO MUSIC* (2020)

NEAR AND DEAR

Some things are near but not dear.
Some things are dear but not near.
Only two things are both near and dear.
One is the thing you most love.
The other is the thing you most hate.

BOURBON

It may not be
the be-all and end-all,
but it is the inbetween-all.

NOW THAT

Now that the ash tree
is cut down and out of
the way, the new
light can light
the way for new trees
to come in that way.

CONQUEST CONQUERS ALL

There is only one Mt. Everest.
But that doesn't stop them.
There is only one tallest in the world.
So that is the only prize worth prizing.
There is only one Mt. Everest.
Of Mt. Everests there is only one.

DISNEY

He hated Jews.
I hated Mickey Mouse.
We were even.

THE CLOUDBURST

The cloudburst was brief
but broke heat's choke
hold long enough to let
the cooler air exhale.

AND THEN IN THE ARMS
OF THE GALAXY WITH THE SPIRAL ARMS

And then I shall spiral out of control.
And then I shall sing the sad cradle song.
And then I shall spiral out of control.
And then I shall sing the sad love song.
And then I shall spiral out of control.
And then I shall sing the sad funeral dirge.
And then I shall spiral in the arms of the galaxy with
the spiral arms.

AUGUSTULUS

Someone had to be last.
Someone had to close the door behind him.
Someone had to break the last sword in half.
Someone had to burn all the secrets.
Someone had to ride the last horse away.
Someone had to take the fall for the fall.

A PEN MAKES A GOOD DRUMSTICK

You can drum the whiskey glass with it.
You can drum the metal flower-shaped table with it.
You can drum the telephone with it.
You can drum away the seconds with it.
You can drum away the minutes with it.
You can drum away the poem with it.
You can beat the drum to beat the drum with it.
You can beat the devil with it.

IF RIGHT NOW

If right now left
now,
right now
would still be left
right now.

NEGLECT

The neglected pool behind
the neglected fence beside
the neglected house is full
of what the trees, of what
the raccoons, of what the weeds,
of what the geese have not neglected.

THREE BARNS

Even in collapse, they
are different in decay.
Each has its own way
of going down, of giving
ground to ground. This
one's roof is gone. That
one's covered but falls
into the space of the missing
wall. And that one is roof,
and that's all.

from **YEARS LATER** (2021)

THE ATTIRE OF THE FREQUENT FLIER
SCREAMED ESQUIRE

I wanted to stick out my leg.
I wanted to trip him.
He had a big mustache.
He had a big wallet full of cash.
He bought a coffee and a bagel.
He paid with a hundred dollar bill.
He took no change.
He left it all as tip.
Bless his soul, but still.
But still I wanted to ruin his trip.

HE WAS ALREADY THERE BEFORE I WAS THERE

He was already singing.
He was already seated in his solid silver chair.
But I got there just in time.
But just in time I pulled up a silver plated chair.
I was always the next to tallest.
I was always the next to best.

I DIDN'T GO THIS MORNING

So I spent the morning not going.
I didn't do it this afternoon.
So I spent the afternoon not doing it.
I didn't listen to it this evening.
So I spent the evening not listening to it.
But this morning was well-spent.
And this afternoon was well-spent.
And this evening was well-spent.
All day I got my money's worth.

CUPID AND PSYCHE

Cupidity and Psychology
fornicated on a cloud.
And that's how the twins
Cupidology and Psychidity were born.

PHANTOM LIMBS

I used to have two lilacs.
They died and are no more.
Yet still I smell lilac in the yard.
But this only when I close my eyes.
This is only when I inhale too deeply
for the breath of ordinary breathing.

ICE

The ice thawing
on the lake sings
as it turns back
to water again
a song neither
happy nor sad
but just a simple
wordless tune
for going home.

UNDER THE LEAVES

I blew off the walkway,
the worms wormed their
way out differently from
the way they wormed
their way in.

THE SKY

The sky, mostly blue
but not entirely, is,
nevertheless, a pure
sky for which the clouds
do not diminish but replenish
with timorous temerity
its integrity.

MAGNOLIA

I can already see, even
now in February, how
magnanimous the magnolia
is going to be. I can already
see it will give away thousands,
thousands so magnificently!

THE STORY

It was so quiet today
the only sound was
my neighbor's washing
machine spinning
a story of falling over
falls head over heels.

UNHAPPILY NEVER BEFORE

They danced down the aisle.
They sang up the smile.
They dance more than a mile.
They sang without guile.
They danced without style.
They sang in single file.
They danced and danced before the trial.
They sang and sang all the while.

TWO SPIDERS

Whitman's is okay.
It's noiseless.
It's patient.
It's the soul of a poet.
But Dickinson's is better.
It crawls around her ass.
It chases her from the outhouse.
It's the body and soul of a poet.

FLAG

Flailing first, then flung out in the wind,
my neighbor's flag flaps
on one wing perpendicular to its pole,
a filibuster of red, white, and blue.

POSITIVELY NEGATIVELY CAPABLE

The odes are not for me.
The sonnets are all right.
But my favorite is "La Belle Dame sans Merci."
I knew one once who had me in thrall.
She was more than all right.
Alas, she was not for me.
That's all.

OBVERSE OBSERVED

It's not obvious at first,
the barbed wire shadow,
but a moment into it,
you begin to make out
how the outline falls in line
around the shadow in reverse,
oblivious to the ground.

COLD SNAP

Yellowing, the forsythia
have not foreseen it,
this spring cold snap, but
the daffodils, holding in
abeyance their yellow still
still below, have.

THE WHIRLWIND

The whirlwind hoists
the dried leaves
fallen from fall then
coughs them up,
rough, on the asphalt,
a dry cough in the
whirlwind's voice.

STRICKEN

I am struck by how many
times I'm stuck in thought's
same place. It's as though
someone is out to get me,
someone strangely stuck on me.

YEARS

A bonsai forest,
the moss of decades
cascades over
the stone wall
to nearly cover it.

THE JET

The jet leaves
this sky over
here for that sky
over there, sucking
in this sky over here
to leave it in that
sky over there.

THE SUN, THE SKY, THE MOURNING DOVE

The sun sings the old song
of the sky.
The sky sings the old song
of the mourning dove.
The mourning dove sings the old song
of the new mourning dove.

EMPHASIS IS ALL

Life is not
like that.
Life is like
that.

I FOLLOWED THE SUN

I followed the sun around
this afternoon. I moved
my chair from the back to
the side to the front to stay
in the sun. I needed the sun
that much. I needed the sun
that badly. I needed the sun
for that long.

THANKSGIVING

The math of myth is all it is.
They're all the same,
the holidays, the holy days.
They're wholly lies.
The math of myth is all they are.
Each passing year another layer
for the liar in you, just another number
added to the math of myth.

SAINT STONE

Once a man named Stone
had a plan of his very own
to become a saint by simply
painting his face and hands
with silver paint. So he spent
his fortune on silver paint
and painted his face and hands,
and now he is known as Saint
Stone all over the place.

from **THE DUST** (2021)

NAMES

There are too many names.
Too much is named.
Eve should have been deaf and dumb.
And blind, too.
Not each and every thing needs a name.
Blessed are the anonymous for they shall inherit the
earth.

WHERE BIG HOUSES NOW ARE

Where big houses now are,
so ugly, so ugly, there were
cornfields, and scarecrows
stood in the cornfields, and
while I miss the cornfields,
I miss the scarecrows more.

JEALOUSY

Does the purple crocus know
that it is the first to burst
right through the dead leaves?
No, but the forsythia does.
Just see how it scratches my
arm as I bend to smile at them.

THERE IS AN INSISTENT GREEN

There is an insistent green
now that the snow is gone,
but even yesterday, I saw
the ditch grass poke its thumb
in winter's half-closed icy eye.

DEAF CHILD AREA

I slow down and look around
whenever I drive by the house,
not knowing what I expect to
see exactly except a child at
a window waving. I really would
like to see that one day. Just once.
So I could wave back. Just once.

IN CASE

In case you have
no soul, it is your
heart you must sell
to the devil.

IN THE GEORGIA O'KEEFFE MUSEUM, SANTA FE

I asked my eight-year old daughter
what she thought of *Part of the Cliffs*
and of the photograph of the site for
Part of the Cliffs, which was on the wall
next to it. "The photograph is what she
saw with her eyes open. The painting
is what she saw with her eyes closed,"
she said.

SOUL

The valley has a soul.
The valley's soul is the river.
But the river because it is a soul, doesn't have one.
Which do you wish to be?
Do you wish to be a soul or to have one?
Do you wish to be the valley or the river?
Or do you wish to be the mountain above the valley,
above the river, the very soul of above it all?

REQUEST

When the man in the next room
died, his daughter gave his flowers
to the nurses, so Emily, my daughter,
listen to me. When I am the man
in the next room, give my flowers
to the homeliest nurse only.

OPINIONS

The carpenter working at
the new house on Shore Drive
is listening to his boom box.
It's very loud. But it's Muddy
Waters, so I have changed my
mind about carpenters.

I WAS LOOKING FOR THE IMPORTANT ONE

I looked in the drawers. I looked in the closets.
I looked in the pantry. I looked under the kitchen
sink. I looked under the bathroom sinks. I looked
in the attic. I looked in the basement. I looked in
the garage. I looked on the book shelves. I looked
in my pockets. I looked everywhere for the important
one. I finally found it. It was in the trash can. It was
under all the other important ones.

THE SAXOPHONE PLAYER

The saxophone player was sitting
on a park bench in the bright sun
playing, "Somewhere Over the
Rainbow." He wasn't very good,
so I guess that's why he was playing
it over and over. I didn't mind. I like that
tune, especially on a park bench,
the sun glinting on a golden saxophone.

from **LIFE-SIZE** (2021)

LIFE-SIZE

Nature abhors a panorama.
The snowflake is in the cherry blossom.
The gnat is in the eagle's wing.
Make yourself small.
Then make yourself smaller.
Then make yourself life-size.

GRAVITY

Graves are
not exempt
even though
they're in
the family.

CONSCIOUSNESS

Let them get off on it,
the philosophers, the physicists.
Let them get it on,
the Buddhists, the neuroscientists.
All I need to know is
how to turn it off and turn it on again.

IMPROVEMENTS

I could make them if I chose to.
I could add this.
I could subtract that.
I could change this color.
I could change that shape.
Or I could leave well enough alone,
which is how well enough has always been left.

RADIANT CONNECTIONS

Ammons, these afternoons,
when the shadows lengthen
and widen, the sun still makes
its slender connections that reach
to brush the cheeks of the trees
on the far end of the lawn.

ZENISH

As long as it never
becomes total
selflessness, I'm
just fine with
less self the better.

CACOPHONY

It was all the birds
all the time until
my neighbor's log
splitter kicked in
and kicked them out.

WHAT THE EARTH SAYS

The earth says, Have a place.
The earth says, I have many.
The earth says, I have more than enough for all of you.
The earth says, But listen carefully.
The earth says, Do not call it your own.
The earth says, Especially your final resting place.
The earth says, That especially do not call your own.

FOR SAMUEL MENASHE

What took you years took me
an hour. Therefore, we must agree
that time does not exist,
or that it does—with a devilish twist.

LUST

It drives desire mad as the whip
does horses. It drives the grasses
and all green things mad for the sun.
It drives men and women wild
for each other. There is no other
word for it except, Must!

RELIGION

It was not a difficult
decision to leave my
religion. Yahweh made
it easy by doing things
his way.

ASHES

In place of fire
in the fireplace,
where heat at
hearth's heart was,
colder than memory,
ashes are.

RUINS

Stones first come to mind.
Then wood. Then iron. Then glass.
Then finally the mind, which
no longer knows the place of
glass, of iron, of wood, of stone,
comes to mind.

THE FREIGHT

What a horn of mournful
warning it sounds as it nears
the crossing as though it
has already killed you.

IT

What do we
need to make
of it to make
of it?

from *IT'S ABOUT TIME* (2022)

HOUR

I want to name
this hour, this hour
I live in now neither
witching nor happy,
neither children's
nor lunch, neither
darkest nor zero.
I want to name this
hour, this hour that
I die in now, the wasted.

SHADOWS

There are many shadows
on the ground, but only
one shadow moves. It is
the shadow of the hawk,
which is as silent as the hawk
that makes it while waiting
for the ground to move.

YOSEMITE

Was it a crow or a raven
that flew down from the pine
to the ground beside me?
It doesn't matter to me,
but to the one who finds
the feather, it is everything.

THE TREE OF KNOWLEDGE

The only knowledge
stored in the apple core
was the knowledge of good
and evil, of nakedness and sex.
Whether it knew the origin
of the universe is not recorded.

IMMENSITY

I looked up into
the immensity
of the sky just at
the right moment
to see the hawk
traverse the immense
city of the clouds.

HYDRANGEAS

I forgot about them.
It has been a year, after all.
What do you remember after
a year? But here they are again
in their corner of the garden,
bigger than ever, which I take
to mean, in the language
of hydrangeas, *Better.*

THE SOUL'S SEA

I don't believe you
have to believe in it
to sail on the sea of
yourself. Look at me,
Ammons. I'm doing
it, and I can't swim.

INCIDENCE

A crow came flying
from a tree in front of me,
arc-turned right up higher
back into the same tree
while a second crow
came flying down,
tracing the same arc
left, which, because both
occurred in one eye-blink,
I call one incidence.

FOUND IN TRANSLATION

Whenever I write a bad poem,
I send it to my friend, Francisco,
in Portugal, who sends it right
back, and which, although
I cannot read it, I know is so
much better in Portuguese.
I must make more foreign friends.

PANTOMIME

A small private plane
flew overhead.
I thought it was
the Angel of Death,
so I waved,
and it dipped its wings.

AUGUST ALE

Did you see the light blonde light
at the end of the tunnel?
So did you enter the tunnel and tunnel
through all the way until
the tunnel turned into a funnel
through which the light turned into a female
with golden cheeks and golden cheeks?

THE GOVERNOR OF POETRY

Of course, she was a woman.
Of course, she was a Democrat.
Of course, you donated to her campaign.
Of course, you made telephone calls on her behalf.
Of course, you went door-to-door on her behalf.
Of course, she lost, Alfred.

A DAY OF DESPAIR

It's the laughingstock
of the deep sea, you say,
Alfred, and I believe you,
for I hear the deep wind
laughing at my despair,
the deep wind which is
the identical twin
of the deep sea.

IMPATIENS

Shameless, how
they fool the shade
into believing
it's the sun.

INTRODUCTIONS

It's good to know about
them before you dive
in, I suppose. I guess it's
helpful to be prepared, but
I never read them. You'll
know right away how warm
or how cold the water is.

MARY O'ROONEY

What is it about the colleens, Alfred?
What is it?
Oh, what is it about the colleens that attracts us so?
Is it their red hair?
Is it their green eyes?
Is it their bewitching smiles?
Is it the miles they make us walk on our knees?
Is it the poems they make us talk?
Or is it the whiskies?

WILDERNESS

What is the minimal wild for a wilderness?
There are acres here behind houses
where no one ever goes, so are these acres wilderness?
What of the one behind mine where I never go?
Is that wilderness?
How many trees do there have to be?
How many trees rotting on the ground?
How many owls?

ROBIN HOOD

Was his name Robin Hood because he wore a hood?
Was his name Robin Hood because he hid in the forest?
Was his name Robin Hood because "Robin the Good"
would have been too obvious?
That doesn't matter.
Here's what matters.
Errol Flynn was too old.

TWO MIRACLES

Your cardinal was in the bush, Alfred.
Mine was in the birdbath.
Yours was burning.
Mine was turning water to wine.

REGRET

Chris, my colleague in the music department,
said he was going to set one of my poems to music.
He wanted to do it for chorus.
He never did.
What a shame.
I was looking forward to getting an erection
watching the sopranos and the altos
with their mouths around my words,
blowing them way up into the balcony where I sit.

NEIGHBOR

One of my neighbors had three horses.
One of them died, leaving two.
A second horse died, so one was left.
Eventually, that one died, leaving none.
I used to call him "neighbor with three horses."
After that I called him "neighbor with two horses."
Finally, I called him "the neighbor with a horse."
Now he's "that neighbor with the messy,
        overgrown meadow."

IT MAKES NO DIFFERENCE TO THE EARTH

It makes no difference to the earth
whether you sit or stand up straight,
whether you lie on your back
or lie on your stomach,
whether you walk or you crawl or you run.
It takes you where you need to go.
It takes you there.
It takes you home.

NURSE

I want a nurse. I've always wanted to marry a nurse.
I still want to marry a nurse.
What man would not want a nurse as a wife?
Do you think a doctor would not? I am not a doctor.
I want a nurse. I would not take advantage of her.
I would not pretend to be ill. She shall not minister
        to me that way.
I want a nurse. And I know the nurse I want.
She was the tall one. She was the slender one.
She was the one who laughed at my skinny legs.
She was the one who winked at me as I left
        the hospital.

A SMILE

A smile is the flower of a laugh.
A laugh is the fruit of a smile.
You can pick a laugh from the tree of a face.
You can taste how sweet it is.
You must respect a smile.
You must not disturb a smile.
A smile is more fragile than a laugh.
You must wait.
You must wait for the smile to ripen.
You must wait for it to fall from the face of its own
        weight.

ANNIVERSARY

I knew the man in charge of all the funerals at the NYPD.
"How do you do it?" I asked him.
"It's my job. I'm in charge of all the funerals," he said.
"I understand. But how do you do it?" I said.
"Isn't this the life?" he said while looking at his pool.
I looked at his pool.
It was bluer than the sky.
"Do you have a pool?" he said.

JACOB

Jacob could not have been
the only one to wrestle
with an angel. I mean,
there must have been many,
hundreds of those desert dwellers
who did. And many more,
thousands, who did one better,
who fucked the angels all night long
on the tent's carpeted floor.

THE WHISKEY

spilled on the
table takes a long
time to evaporate.
The sun is thirstier
than I am.
It won't be long.

from **COMING TO** (2022)

THE SNOW

The snow was so completely
deep, so deeply complete,
the world was so winsome
in white, I thought it was
making itself a virgin again.

MARCH

The sun shines softly.
The snow melts slowly.
The lone crow wipes
its small wings on
the wide white of the lake.

THE SNOW MELTS

The icy water rushes down
to the road ditch and through
the long culvert, which was
the plan all along.

CORROBORATION

Amazing how still
the bourbon in the glass
remains given how fast
the universe is accelerating
from itself, Ammons.

BLUE SKIES AGAIN

I look, Ammons, but
I do not leap. It is just
as blue down here even
though you cannot see
it for the green.

POETRY TO THE RESCUE AGAIN

Even if what we hear
is only the clip-clop
clip-clop of coconuts
cut in half, it's still
the cavalry, right,
Ammons?

SCARAMENT SACRAMENT

It was in a poem about
going to church. It was
the most frightening
typographical error
I ever saw.

NEIGHBORLY

My neighbor is burning
something. I think they
are leaves. It doesn't matter
what he is burning. The smoke
is heavy and dark. It rises over
the outcropping between our houses,
a visible stench as foul as a rumor.

CORNELL

After the beautiful young
woman walked past me in
the other direction, a young
man came along. "If you
hurry, you might catch up
with her," I said pointing to
the young woman as she
disappeared between buildings.
Was I being impertinent?
Not if it paid off.

SWIMMING LESSON

I push the pen
into the deep end,
so deep, it can't
see the bottom.

AMBITION

After a day of doing
nearly nothing,
I vowed to do better
the next time.

TODAY

Today the sky was cloudlessly
so blue, it was the blunt
end of bland, but still it
gestured earthward grander
than any grand gesture
down here.

THE BEE

The bee met me at
the mountain laurel,
softly feeling out
the flowers' undersides
too small for it, but there
were no hard feelings
on either side.

HAPPINESS

Why do the daffodils, erect,
up to their waists in the water
of the vase look happier than
they did in the ground? Should
I ask, my friend, Jim, the philosopher
or my friend, Emil, the biologist?

from **THE DREAMS OF THE GODS** (2023)

AMBIGUITY

When the wind picked up,
it kicked up all the leaves
raking up missed in the fall,
but the rake is stowed away
to stay for spring's sake,
so the leaves are free to go.

THE CLOUDS

The clouds know all the grays,
display them one by one.
The sun doesn't stand a chance,
but the cherry stands its ground
to put its blossoms out,
sunlessly grayfully all the same.

THE NICKEL

It should not have the tail.
It should have the real tale.
It should show the two Jeffersons.
It should show the Declaration Jefferson.
It should show the slaver Jefferson.
The nickel should be two-faced like Jefferson.

EASTER

Hey, Yeshua, it's been
two millennia in heaven.
Come back. All is forgiven.

AFTER THE READING

A women came up to me.
"I like a lot of your poems.
But I have to say that some
of them seem more like ghosts
of poems than real poems,"
she said. Then she walked away
without giving me the benefit
of knowing which were which.

THE BEST MYTHS ARE THE METAMORPHOSES

The best are the ones who change,
transform, shift shapes from one
ordinary to one more strange,
from one merely mortally to one
there immortally, from a moon-
faced lover to the lover of the moon.

MEDEA IS THE MESSAGE

"Take that," she said.
"Take that and that and that," she said.
But that was not enough for her.
So she recorded it for us.
"Take this," she says.
"Take this and this and this," she says forever.

SWAMP

As I walked by,
two of the three
turtles sunbathing
on a log sensed a
threat so slid in while
the third stayed put,
somehow knowing
I was only a poet.

DEDICATION

I want what he got,
Hippolytus, not the life,
not the death, but after
that godawful mess,
the way the maidens,
before they married, cut
off a lock of hair for
him in dedication with
such loving tenderness.

THE DIFFERENCE

I have not lost my mind.
I have loosed my mind.
You will find there's
a difference. One or the
other will someday make
sense. One or the other
will someday be the ghost.

THREE THINGS I KNOW FOR SURE

I know I am free to do anything I wish.
I know I am not free to do anything I wish.
I know this is not ironic.

THE SHADOW

The shadow of a hawk
passed through my
shadow as I walked
around the lake. One
day a hawk's shadow
will take my shadow
with it to its high place
it has found for us.

BLEEDING HEARTS

On the phone, 96-year-old
Eva says it's too early for
bleeding hearts to bloom
while I am looking at mine
bloom in the garden, but
I don't have the heart
to tell her.

IF THE EYE COULD WRITE

it would tell exactly what it sees.
If the lips could see,
they would swear them all to secrecy.

SUNFLOWERS

They always face the sun.
I have seen them, so I know.
When there is no sun, they face one another.
I have not seen this, but I have heard this is true.
I believe it.
I would believe anything sunflowers do.

WITHOUT APOLOGIES

I have a wheelbarrow.
It isn't red.
Not much depends on it.
I don't have chickens.
My neighbor has chickens.
They make a mess of my mulch.
They shit like crazy on my walk.
I wish it would rain.

BAR TALK

"I'd give anything for
the love of one good
woman," he said. "Or
one good woman and
two bad ones," said
the other.

I WANT THE GODS TO EXIST

I want them to exist just for one day.
One hour will be all I need.
I want to insult one to her face.
I want to insult her so she could turn me into
something.
Turn me into a tree, or a flower, or best of all, a rock.
A rock on the coastline of an island in the Aegean.
A rock famous for its shape of a man
with a mysterious smile on his face.

TIE

I learned how to tie a full Windsor
knot from my father. The full
Windsor was more complex than
the half Windsor. It required more
overs and more unders. I practiced
it over and over until I mastered it.
I learned it by heart as things worth
learning are learned. I learned it
for his funeral. I learned it for hers.

THE SHIELD OF HECTOR

The shield of Hector
was not much to see,
just bronze and leather,
so unlike that of Achilles,
the great masterpiece
Hephaestus made,
but Hector's stained shield
smelled of the sweat he shed
in battle and was used to carry
his son, Astyanax, dead
from Troy and was the coffin
he was buried in.

THE WHITE PEONIES EXPLODE

"Why are you so angry?" I ask.
"We are not angry. We cannot contain
 our sexual energy," they answer.
"But you are almost as old as I am.
 When I explode nowadays, it is from anger," I say.
"We are flowers," they say.
"Be thankful you are flowers and not men," I say.
"Oh, we are. We assure you, we are," they exclaim.

from **ALONE** (2023)

DEAD WISTERIA

Wistful for its
former flowering,
it holds on in
petrified hysteria.

SLIPPER

It was a slip-up, those glass
slip-ons, the translator's
error using the *verre* of glass
for the *vair* of fur, but felicitous
for her whose feet fit such shoes
only true heroines could wear.

UNSONNET TO ORPHEUS

Oh, shit.
Don't you see
that only gods may sing
so beautifully
and get away with it?
You idiot!

HAIR AND MUD

Socrates said not all things
partake of Plato's Ideal.
For instance, there is no hair
and mud in his Up There.
The gods, it seems, are bald,
and they stroll on roads of gold.

FOUR CHAIRS

Around the table,
there are four chairs.
I sit in one. The other
three are for only
those three friends
who will not, under
any circumstances,
give me their advice.

THE STONE WALL

I built years ago
has disappeared
beneath the tall
green laugh of
the weedful grass.

WISDOM

It's never comfortable standing.
It always needs a chair.
Or a tree stump.
Or a boulder.
Or a marble stair.
It always needs a space at its feet
for the wide-eyed to stare.

THE EARS

They see all, so much
more than the eyes.
The ears have the x-ray
vision the eyes only
dream of. The ears see
in back of your head
as though you have eyes
in the back of your head.

SWEET

Too much is cloying.
Like too much sex.
One climax too many.
One anticlimax already
too many. Leave half
the whipped cream in
the dish. Leave half
the coffee in the cup.

ADVICE

I remember his advice.
"Fish or cut bait," he said.
I cut bait so many times
the fish felt sorry for me.

A MEMORY

Lining up in size place
in the hallway, boys on
one side, girls on the other,
for fingernail inspection
before marching into the
classroom, must be true,
for my mind would never
make up fingernail inspection.

"ENGLISH IS THE LANGUAGE OF HELL..."
—HAYDEN CARRUTH

I always thought it was German,
but I see your point, Hayden,
those mass murderers, Napoleon,
N'Kruma, Alcibiedes, Truman,
sitting around drinking bourbon
down there, but I still vote for German,
and if you were a Jew, you'd know what I mean.

THE DEAD

They live so long, the dead.
They live so much longer than
the living do. They live forever,
the dead. Tell me, is it fair?
Is it fair for the dead to live forever
while the living live for no time
at all? Is it fucking fair?

ASH TREE STUMP

Grass grows out of it now,
already higher than the lawn
around it, but I had to prune
back the hop hornbeam, for
it was out of control, maniacal,
wildly waving its arms around
around its newfound universe.

from **LEDA** (2023)

AFTER THE RAIN

After the rain and the wind,
the sky comes again, the
blue one, the one we think
of when we think sky, the one
accompanied by clouds
we think of when we think
clouds, the white, the new,
the virginal, the brides.

STRAIGHT TALK

So I talked to God
who ended it with a wink
but not with a nod.

THE WORDS

They must meet me on my terms.
They must come alone.
They must come in good faith.
They must be hungry.
They must have fasted for days.
They must be all skin and bone.
They must beg for food and water.
They must beg for forgiveness.
They must beg for their lives.

MONSTERS ARE NOT
ALWAYS MISUNDERSTOOD

Some we understand very well.
A few we understand all too well.
We understand what they want to tell
us, the sob story of their homelife's living hell.
We understand why they stop to yell
at us to buy what they're trying to sell,
to fall for how far from grace they supposedly fell.

I WAS AT THE BAR

I was at the bar having my
second beer when an old guy
sat down. He asked for a
double Irish whiskey, neat.
"That'll warm the cockles of
your heart," I said. "Yes, but
it's the heart of my cockles
I want warmed," he said.
"Cheers," I said "Cheers,"
he said and downed it in
the blink of an eye.

THE VALLEYS OF THE YOUNG,
THE MOUNTAINS OF THE OLD

The old want to meet the young.
They come down from their mountains to the valley.
The young, however, do not want to meet the old.
Neither do they want to climb the mountain.
They move to the next valley too far for the old to find.

A DRAGONFLY

A dragonfly flies
on wings of windows
through which
the sky is
always seen
to be at home.

THE PERFECT POET

A four-year-old has published
a book of poetry. His name is
Nadim Shamma. One of his best
is, "Everyone has love/Even
baddies." He dictates his poems
to his mamma. He's the perfect
poet. You know he'll grow up
before he'll blow it.

SHORT SPEECH FOR HADES

Zeus is a part-time seducer.
I'm the one with the full-time lust.
I'm the number one reducer
of mortals to shadow and dust.

EPIMETHEUS

He was the brother of Prometheus.
He was the husband of Pandora.
She was the first woman.
She was the one who opened the box
to release all the evils into the world.
Some say it was Epimetheus who did
because he had the key and not her.
It doesn't matter. It was done.
But it's always a better story when
the woman's the disobedient one.

THE DEDUCTION FROM THE ABDUCTION

The deduction from the abduction is not seduction.
That does not work in art.
Art requires bodies in motion.
Or one body part against another.
Especially the sculptor shows his skill
with stone by seizing the terrified against her will.
Only in the midst of violence
does the stony silence make sense.

ANOTHER SHORT SPEECH FOR HADES

Gentlemen and Ladies,
I am Hades.
A good tune
makes me swoon,
but why oh, why do they
always disobey?

AUGUST

The hydrangea claims
the garden's corner
where they make white
where only green was,
each cluster a fist
defiant in the face
of chlorophyll.

SPACE

Space is so spacious
but not spacious enough
for two galaxies to seize
their chance to fall
into one another's arms.

THE CHAIR OF FIRE

After the fire, the only thing
I kept was a chair, burn-
blackened, flame-charred,
smoke-smoldered. I will not
get rid of this chair, this
chair of fire, this poetry chair.

JUXTAPOSITION

The white butterfly
by being on the
marigold makes
the flower yellower
while opening its
wings, the butterfly
on the flower gets
white whiter.

THE MOON

I have a friend, a poet,
who dedicated her last
book to the moon. "Why
did you do that, Cathryn?"
I asked. "Because the
moon is our closest neighbor
and most steadfast friend,"
she said. "That's not the moon
I know," I said to myself.

MY NEIGHBOR

Because he keeps chickens for eggs,
taps the maples for syrup, hunts
deer and turkey for meat, and
cuts and splits wood for warmth,
he thinks he's self-sufficient,
but he still gets his music from
the radio instead of a player piano.

THE BOAST

Jim and I were at the bar
when a woman turned
to us and said, "I can
drink the both of you
under the table with one
eye tied behind my back."
Hell, she wasn't even drunk.

I ADMIRE THE LAST ONES

I admire the holdouts that hold on until the very end.
I admire the ones who linger long after all the
       others have left.
I admire the last to leave, the ones who cannot take
       the hint.
I admire their stubbornness.
I admire their foolishness that looks like love.

from **THE EGLANTINE** (2023)

AFTER A MORNING

After a morning of overcast,
the sun cast itself over
the clouds long enough
to light up noon,
then went undercover
again to spy on the afternoon.

AFTER THE EARLY

After the early frost of
overnight, the marigolds
lost some, but some more
still held their own
still holding their own.

TODAY THE SKY WAS TWO SKIES

There was the blue sky with white clouds.
There was the overcast gray sky next to it.
It was a civil war of sorts of skies.
The thunder from the south was the first shot fired.

MARRIAGE

"Marriage is a prison," she said.
She was my friend's second wife.
"But you've been married for only
two years," I said. "That's long
enough to know," she said. She
ought to know. This was her third.
I guess not all prisons are the same.

BARKING

My neighbor's dog is barking.
It is a loud, deep, confident bark.
It is the bark of an animal that knows who it is.
I'd like to bark like that.
I would bark at everyone and everything.
I would be the best damn barker in the neighborhood.
I would bark up every tree, right or wrong.
My bark would be my bite.

OCTOBER IS NOT SOBER

It's the drunkard of the year.
It sees pink elephants in the orange oaks.
It stumbles along the red road.
It falls on its face.
It falls some more.
It slurs its speech.
Its speech is colorful even slurred.
It is intoxicated on dying marigolds, yellower than ever.

OCTOBER DOES NOT LAST LONG ENOUGH

It should be the longest of the year.
It has the most to offer.
September should move over.
November should move over.
They should let October elbow them aside.
September and November should defer to October.
September should give ten days to October.
November should give ten days to October.

MY NEIGHBOR

My neighbor is
playing with her
dog. She is making
strange sounds
I cannot spell.

LEAVES

A strong gust of wind
has shot so many
yellow leaves off
the trees in one shot,
I thought the sun had
shorted out and shattered
itself against the sharp
cloud-rocks.

WALK

On my walk by the marsh,
I heard the cry of a red-winged
blackbird. By the time I walked
back, I had learned it by heart.
Why not? It was the cry of
the only bird in the marsh
all that time.

from *THE BOOK OF A SMALL FISHERMAN* (2023)

NO WONDER

There may
have been.
But there surely
isn't anymore.

FLASH FLOOD

A few drops of rain,
not even enough to
chase me inside,
but a moth on the
desert of a hosta leaf
has found its oasis.

OMEN

"Why do you not heed,
oh, women, oh, men?"
saith the crow flying
loud and flying low out
of the white cloud.

NO LAND

No land should be
promised. No stone
should be bound by laws.
No bush should burn,
and no whirlwind speak
in any voice but its own.
No good, no good can come
of any miracle.

BEOWULF

Yes, it is long.
Yes, it is boring.
But, holy shit,
it's the greatest
long, boring
poem there is.

CIRCUS

I remember the stallion smells.
I remember the elephant smells.
I remember the clown smells.
I remember the trapeze smells.
I remember the sawdust smells.
I remember the Fat Lady's Queen of Smells.

WILLIAM BLAKE

For heaven's sake,
how could you be
both so right and so
wrong in one little
song, William Blake?

NO DESIGN

Although a darning needle
balances on the tip
of a tall weed stalk,
there is no design,
and that's just fine with me.

SHYLOCK

Shakespeare's only
villainous Jewish villain
doesn't die. No, his fate
is worse than death,
this Job whose daughter
and whose wealth
are not restored.

THE EYES OF MY APPLE

When I cut into my apple,
I see its five eyes staring back at me.
They are black like the eyes of gypsies.
When I bite into my apple, I spit out
its black eyes so as not to swallow
the eyes of gypsies.
It's bad luck.

ARTHRITIS

It's everywhere, but the right wrist
has the worst of it. My doctor says
it's only right since that's the joint
we use the most, and "for you right-
handed poets, that's the cost."

ON THE RADIO

They were talking about
the origin of the universe.
One said, "Science." One
said, "Miracle." One said,
"The miracle of science."
Then there was silence.

LATIN

Pope of languages,
everything is official
in it. It's the last word,
the final, infallible authority.
O tempora! O mores! it intones.
Pulvis et umbra sumus,
it pontificates from its throne.

MEDUSA

Monstrously misunderstood,
she was the giver of good,
for she granted the immortality
all men crave, the monument
of stone atop their grave.

CATCH

Ammons, when I first read
your "Catch," I thought
it was my catch, but it was
the other one, the one about
the chimney flue and the moon.
Or was that the catch I didn't catch?
As we know so well,
there's one to everything.

ISAAC

That night, he had
a terrible dream.
The Angel of the Lord
appeared to him and said,
"Isaac, wake your father,
Abraham."

TYPO

The most
mischievous
of the Marx
Brothers.

TRAGEDY

It's about the door
with the broken bell.
It's about the window
facing the street stuck shut.
It's about that and nothing more.
Oh, it's also about hell.

APPOINTMENT

Thanks, doc.
I'll keep you posted
if I can keep her
posted or not.

WASTE

I know better than to believe
that the trees masturbated all
these seeds onto the ground,
but wouldn't it be a real shame
if they didn't get at least some
pleasure out of all this waste?

BEACHED BOAT

The small rowboat,
face-down on the ground,
chained to a tree, now
floats in place upon
the earth along with
everything else on earth.

HONESTY

Honestly, there's something
to be said for honesty.
It's the alpha and the omega
of how we talk, you and me.
It's better than lying to each other,
but you must admit, dear friend,
it causes more trouble in the end.

WASHINGTON D. C.

The flagpole
in front of the EPA
was rusty.

MY NEIGHBOR'S BUDDHAS

My neighbor has Buddhas on her lawn.
She has a lot of Buddhas on her lawn. I must
have counted nine or ten Buddhas on her lawn.
There are large Buddhas, small Buddhas, tall
Buddhas, short Buddhas, sitting Buddhas, standing
Buddhas, sleeping Buddhas, dancing Buddhas, stone
Buddhas, wooden Buddhas. The fat laughing Buddha
under the American flag is my favorite.

MEMORY

Every old man has one. This one is mine.
It was Washington Square Park.
It was summer. She was wearing a floral print dress.
The dress was white. The flowers were purple and pink.
She looked like a young Ava Gardner. She smiled.
Every old man has one. Ask them. Ask them politely.
Say, "Please," with a little kiss on the cheek.

EPITAPH IN THE FORM OF A SENRYU

Here is what to write:
The bitch of fame barked all night,
but she didn't bite.

SLEEP

Sleep came four times, each time as an older sister.
"Send me your mother," I said to the First Sleep Sister.
"Send me your mother," I said to the Second Sleep Sister.
"Send me your mother," I said to the Third Sleep Sister.
"Send me your mother," I said to the Fourth Sleep Sister.
"Send me the Mother of All Sleep," I said. "Oh, we cannot,"
  they said. "She is dead. She is dead. She is dead. She
  is dead."

VERY SHORT DIALOGUE

"He's so full of himself,"
  the critic said of him.
"Of whom else should I be full?"
  he responded.

DOOR

I painted the front door of my house red.
I chose red because in the Middle Ages
a red door meant sanctuary, a safe place for
thieves, poachers, rebels, and highwaymen,
a haven beyond the reach of the law. I'm not
a thief, a poacher, a rebel or a highwayman,
but I do curse the governor from time to time.

from *GOD* (2024)

WELL, AMMONS, SOMEONE

Well, Ammons, someone
wanted to know who you are,
a librarian, no less, wanted
to know who you are, but why
should I be surprised? There
are librarians, and then there
are librarians.

PEACE

It didn't last long. It never does.
One generation is the most it ever
does, given man's attention span.
The next one, you'll be glad to hear,
Alfred, is shining its boots, sharpening
its bayonet, cleaning and sighting its gun.

LOVE POEM

If he hadn't done
it, I would have.
"She stands in beauty,"
I would have said.
"Her light blonde hair done
up, her eyes blue for the love
of blue, her lips, beguiling,
blushed in softest red,
and her body,
the whole of it, smiling."

I WISH I KNEW MORE PEOPLE

I wish I knew more people,
interesting people,
interesting people to inspire me,
the kind of interesting people you knew, Bill,
to inspire me the way they inspired you.

WISDOM

It is the shadow
that knows the most
about the sun.

THE HAPPINESS OF PURSUIT

On Monday, I pursued the gold of the sun.
On Tuesday, I pursued the silver of the moon.
On Wednesday, I pursued the platinum of the stars.
On Thursday, I pursued the crystals of salt.
On Friday, I pursued the coins of the realm.
On Saturday, I pursued a poem through the woods.
On Sunday, I pursued the widow of the dead future.

CONCERT

Once, twice, the conductor
gave the down beat, but
the chorus, first once, then
twice was late, so for a third
time she began, and all now
kept the music steady until
the last chord, which she
called for longer than the
score called for, twice as long.

WHAT WE KNEW

We knew some things.
Most were not worth knowing.
But we did not know until it was too late.
Isn't that just like us?

COLOR

The scientists say it doesn't exist.
Tell that to the bees.
Tell that to the butterflies.
Tell that to the birds-of-paradise.
Tell that to Mark Rothko.

I HAD ROSES

I had roses.
I have no roses now.
I did not take care of my roses.
My roses were red.
My roses looked spectacular by the yellow lilies.
My roses looked spectacular by the front door.
Of my roses visitors would say, "Your roses look
        spectacular."
This was years ago.
This was about the time my wife got sick.

ULYSSES

What do you know?
Blazes strung old Leo's bow.

AFTER THE READING

After the reading, a woman
came up to me and said, "You
really are a sentimental son-
of-a-bitch, aren't you?" "What
makes you say that?" I asked
"You write about your cats only
when they die," she said.

THE HUMMINGBIRDS ARE GONE

The last one left yesterday.
Godspeed, hummingbirds.
May you arrive safe and sound in Mexico.
Buena suerte, colibríes.
Que llegues sano y salvo a México.
Viva!
Viva, colibries!
Que regresen el próximo año, hermanos y hermanas!

ONCE THERE WAS A CLOUD

Once there was a cloud
that looked like so much
like an angel, it could have
been an angel, for it evaporated
in the wind, which is the way
angels also die.

STAY OUT OF STORES

Stay out of doors if you want to know
the seasons inside and out. Only stay
out of stores, for they will play with
your mind and untune your sense of time
to have you believing in fraudulent years.

from **THEN MORNING** (2024)

EVERY NIGHT

Every night, I ask forgiveness of the world
for leaving it behind, for saying it is not welcome
to go with me into that other place,
that place of dreams where I could be alone,
as far as possible away from it,
but every night the world puts on its mask,
and lights its lamp and follows me there.

DELPHINIUM

Demanding beauty,
it held its breath
until it turned blue,
but is there now not
one god, just one,
to show it mercy
and let it breathe again?

THE LAKE IS A GOOD LISTENER

The lake is a good listener.
It listened to me today when I needed it most.
As I drove around it playing Ellington, it listened
        approvingly.
Its eyes sparkled in the sun.
Its smile was a mile wide.
Its laugh was ninety feet deep.
The great blue heron tapped its foot in its shallows.
O yes, today the lake listened approvingly to my despair.

SNAKE

I saw a dead snake in the middle of the road.
"Oh, I am sorry someone did this to you," I said.
"Don't be. There is neither justice nor mercy in this
        world,"
said the snake. "There is only me in the middle of
        this road,
a road which was not here when my forebears
        divided the grass."

FOR ALL THE WORLD

"A poet looks at the world as a man
 looks at a woman,"
 says Wallace Stevens.
 This is an easy one,
 for the world, like a woman, is a mystery.

THIS MORNING CAME EARLY

This morning came early.
 It had a lot on its mind.
 It needed to unburden itself.
"This better be good," I said.
"O yes, it is. It is good," said the morning.
 It stared at me in silence for what seemed like an eternity.
 It was an eternity.
 It was good.

THIS MORNING WAS DIRTY

This morning was dirty.
 It wanted to be seen clearly.
"I want to be seen clearly," it said to me.
"I can see clearly how dirty you are," I said.

THIS MORNING WAS IN BLACK AND WHITE

This morning was in black and white,
for the night used up
all the color in the world
for the resplendent dreams
of all the world's brand new lovers.

THIS MORNING WAS AN ECHO

This morning was an echo.
It was not mine.
How could it have been?
I had not spoken.

THIS MORNING WAS STALKING ME

This morning was stalking me.
"O, I thought you were
someone else," the morning said.

THIS MORNING WAS THE ANGEL OF DEATH

This morning was the Angel of Death.
It was not mine.
It was a red-tailed hawk.
It was the angel of the field mouse's death.
The field mouse did not complain.
If my Angel of Death is a red-tailed hawk,
I, too, will not complain.

THIS MORNING HAD A HEAVY HEAD

This morning had a heavy head.
It had a very heavy head.
It lay down next to me.
Its eyes were watery and heavy and gray.
They were very watery and very heavy and gray.
It begged for my light hand on its head.
It begged for my blessing.
Of all the hands, it begged for mine.
Of all the blessings, mine.

THIS MORNING CAME IN ITS SUNDAY BEST

This morning came in its Sunday best.
"Where are you off to?" I asked.
"It's Sunday. I'm going to church," the morning said.
"You filthy liar," I said.
"But many people believe me," said the morning.
"That's not my problem," I said.
"No, it's mine," said the morning.

THIS MORNING NOTHING

This morning Nothing
took its rightful place
in my life between
Was and Will Be.

THIS MORNING I HEARD THE WIND

This morning I heard the wind.
No, it was not the wind.
What I heard were wings.
They were the wings of Why.

THIS MORNING WAS NAKED

This morning was naked.
I saw its skin.
Its skin was translucent.
I saw its bones.
Its bones were white.
Its bones were white and heavy and ready
to fall to the earth that was there to welcome them.

THIS MORNING WHISPERED IN MY EAR

This morning whispered in my ear.
"Solonche, you narcissist,
I'm sick and tired of your games," it said.
"So, you've finally learned my name," I said.

THIS MORNING WAS A MIRROR

This morning was a mirror.
"Who is this?" asked the morning.
"I do not know," I said.
"But you knew when it was the night
who asked," said the morning.
"Yes, but the night asked more lovingly
than you ask," I said.

THIS MORNING WEPT

This morning wept.
I did not ask why.
I did not try to comfort it.
I knew why.
For that I knew no comfort.

THIS MORNING THE WORLD WAS A DEAD MOON

This morning the world was a dead moon,
for all the dreams that flew up
to the all the moons
from all the nights fell
back to all the worlds as snow.

THIS MORNING WAS A GOLDEN CUP

This morning was a golden cup.
I drank.
I drank all the way down
to the dregs of dawn.
I drowned
the dream that wanted
to keep the dark up
all around me.

THIS MORNING SAID IT WAS SORRY

This morning said it was sorry.
"Do you apologize for lying
 in the dream you sent in the night?"
I asked this morning.
"No, I apologize for telling the truth
 in the dream I sent in the night," said this morning.

THIS MORNING SPOKE GERMAN

This morning spoke German.
I shut my ears.
Even *Die Sonette an
Orpheus* makes me sick to hear.

THIS MORNING WAS A STORM OF LIGHT

This morning was a storm of light.
After I rubbed thunder from my eyes,
I jumped to my feet
and rushed to the window
to survey the damage the storm
had done to the world that it had aged by a single night.

THIS MORNING WAS A BIRD

This morning was a bird.
It was white and black,
both the white and the black were bright,
with a head of red brighter
than the black or the white,
and the head nodded up and down,
agreeing with everything I said.

THIS MORNING TREES DIED

This morning trees died.
I do not know which trees died
or how many trees died,
but I know that trees died in the woods
this morning.
I know because I heard the wind moan there.

THIS MORNING I DID NOT EXIST

This morning I did not exist.
I disappeared sometime during the night.
It was a full moon, yet I disappeared.
It was a full moon and a clear sky, yet I disappeared.
It was a full moon and a clear sky, yet I couldn't be
      found.
The alarm was raised.
They searched everywhere they could think of, yet
they could not find me.
But they did not search everywhere.
I was where they could not think of.
I was where the full moon told me to go.

THIS MORNING HAD A SECRET

This morning had a secret.
"I will tell you my secret, if you tell me yours,"
  the morning said to me.
"You already know all my secrets,"
  I said to the morning.
"That is too bad, for now you will never know my secret,"
  the morning said to me.

THIS MORNING OPENED MY EYES

This morning opened my eyes.
There was nothing new to see,
 so I closed my eyes.
"Ah, now I see," I said to the morning.
"You opened my eyes to the sameness of the world."

THIS MORNING I WAS A STRANGER TO MYSELF

This morning I was a stranger to myself.
I saw the stranger of myself sitting at my desk.
I was not a stranger to the stranger at my desk.
He knew who I was.
He knew I was the stranger of himself sitting at his desk.
And there was nothing strange about it, for he was
        expecting me.

THIS MORNING I WASTED MY LIFE

This morning I wasted my life.
I wasted it every chance I got.
I wasted it so many times I got very good at it.
I can waste my life at a moment's notice.
I've wasted it hundreds of times.
It is my life.
It is how I live.
It is my daily bread.

THIS MORNING CAME THREE TIMES

This morning came three times.
I wanted nothing to do with the first morning.
I wanted nothing to do with the second morning.
I wanted nothing to do with the third morning.
"You ignored First Morning Sister,"
      said Third Morning Sister.
"You ignored Second Morning Sister,"
      said Third Morning Sister.
"You will not ignore me," said Third Morning Sister.
Then Third Morning Sister took me by the hand and
      led me out into the day.

HORSES

They look sad,
but they are not.
Yet they make
me sad because
they look sad.
It's the fence.

THE UNIVERSE

If the universe goes
on forever, then these
words—which I call
a poem—will go on
forever, too. Do not
misunderstand. This is
not a cause for celebration.

THE LAKE

The water is low, so
low rocks and
the branches of trees
are exposed. Crows
strut where the swans
once swam.

JUPITER

I was up early. It was still dark.
As I passed the window, I saw Jupiter.
It was bright. It was very bright. It was brighter
than any other light in the sky. It was so bright
I forgot everything. I forgot I was at the window.
I forgot I was an old man going to the bathroom.
I forgot what I learned in school about the solar system.
I forgot what I learned about mythology.
I forgot everything except the word, *Jupiter,*
the name of the light brighter than any other light in
the sky.
Then I remembered I was an old man going to the
bathroom.

DEMENTIA

"Such beautiful skin," she said.
"Such soft and beautiful skin," she said.
"What skin lotion do you use?" the visiting nurse said.
"Baby lotion," the caregiver said.
"Oh baby lotion, of course," the visiting nurse said.
"Of course," I said.

HOSPITAL

It's a mountain,
this building, the biggest
in this small city where I come
today to take my neighbor home,
this mountain where when my turn
comes, I will come to climb to die.

I'VE ALWAYS WANTED TO WRITE

I've always wanted to write
a poem on a wall, on
the wall of city hall, or on
the wall of my old high school, or
on the last wall still standing of
a bombed out city, but mostly on
the wall of a temple, as Su Tung-p'o
did when he wrote his poem, "Written on
the Wall at West Forest Temple" in 1084.

WHEN I AM DEAF

When I am deaf and unable to speak,
when I am ready to die
and so unable to go on,
wheel me out into noon's full light
that I may stare up into the sun
long enough to go blind
and thereby give back my eyes
to whatever god it was who created sight.

ON THE PASSING OF CHARLES SIMIC

You said poets can
write on anything,
a toothpick, a rat on
the subways tracks,
a fork, but, Charles,
Charles, I can't write
a poem on your death.

SUPERMARKET

I was waiting on line
at the supermarket, but
I forgot my manners,
so I went back to the
Manners aisle and got
twenty minutes worth.
The cashier was grateful.

BREEZE

Almost too gentle,
the breeze breezes over
the front lawn and
through the bare branches
of the cherry and the magnolia.
Is this what they mean by The Way,
the Daoists? I hope it is, this breeze,
so gentle, almost too gentle, for one to feel the way
        it flows.

DEMENTIA

I tear her favorite French toast
into bite-sized pieces,
I mix them into her favorite
vanilla yogurt with her favorite
spoon, I wipe the excess yogurt
from her mouth with her
favorite pink napkin, I turn up
the volume on her favorite
pianist playing her favorite Bach,
while she looks out of
her favorite window at her
childhood's favorite snow.

DAY LILIES

They no longer appear here,
the day lilies, their speckled orange
throats mouthing the sun's vowels
beside the road. Nothing has dared
take their place. It is as though
the roadside has told the waiting
weeds and drab grasses, "Let us wait.
Let us wait just one more year."

JONES STREET

Except on pick-up days,
ignore each house's false
front front of the forced smiles
of porches. It's the back to best
see where the living is done.

RAILROAD STREET

The railroad tracks over
which no train has traveled
in decades, still in place parallel
to the streets on either side,
tell a silence like no other.
It is the silence of steel rails
remembering steel wheels.

THE LINE

"Why are we dying?"
I read on the back
of the world's left hand
where the world,
not wanting to ever forget,
wrote it to itself.

BIRDBATH

The birdbath has fallen over.
The heavy one made of white stone.
I like it like that, fallen over, the basin upside
down, the tripod on its side. I like the look of it,
an ancient ruin, an ancient Greek, Roman, Egyptian
birdbath for ancient Greek, Roman, Egyptian birds.

ONE RAIL IS LEFT

One rail is left
of the split-rail fence,
the others spilt on
the ground where the grass
climbs all over them.

from **THE ARCHITECT'S HOUSE** (2024)

PANGUR

Awake from his nap on the rug,
My cat, Pangur, his back to me,
opens his eyes, swivels around
to face me, hops up onto the desk,
and anxious for a little monkey
business, puts my scratching black
mouse in his mouth as his mouse
now our mouse.

BLAKE

Blake, how much I would
like to have hailed you in
Lambeth, at No. 13 Hercules
Buildings, sitting naked
in the garden with Catherine.

DAFFODILS

At the stump of the ash tree
cut down years ago,
a clump of daffodils trumpets
its big brass brag: "Look how
powerful we are to fell
this mighty Jericho of trees!"

THE EYE OF A BLINK

What the earth
has taken one
short year to make,
the wind has shaken
down in two
long days.

LEAR

You too, Bill, in yours
recognized the tremendous
absence of the woman,
but whereas I only saw him
as the pathetic, foolish old widower,
you made him wife to the storm,
the female figurehead "at repose
to signify the strength of the waves' lash."

FORTUNATE MEN

If you say you are a fortunate
man, Bill, because the wood
thrush looks at you "silent
without moving," then must
I say I am more fortunate,
for see how the phoebe has
built her nest in the elbow
of the downspout under the gutter,
and more fortunate still as it is
hard by the back door through
which I go in and out many times a day?

CRIMSON AZALEA

Not the first to flower,
does it defer to the forsythia,
the black cherry, the magnolia,
which all get there before?
Does it wait for them to brown
out and drop to have to itself
its singular fire burn against
their green, all the green around?

IRISES

One fully unfolded,
all opened in pale yellow,
a second readying to follow but taller,
they will walk unevenly on the breeze
with the littlest limp on the stage of the earth.

I HAD A TYPEWRITER

All writers of a certain type had one,
By which I mean a certain age.
It was a good editor.
The writing was slow, deliberate, methodical.
So it was a good editor.
You thought of the right word before writing the
        wrong one.
You wrote two lines ahead in your head.
It was stupid.
It was an editor.
It was a frustrated poet.
But it was smart enough to let you be the smart one.
It was smart enough for you.

PEACH TREE

How big it would be now,
the peach tree the winter killed all these years ago.
How many peaches it would have given us,
the tree the snowstorm bent in half,
the tree the ice storm broke completely.
We put an ornamental weeping cherry in its place.

RED-SHOULDERED HAWK

He fell fast from
the tree canopy
in a blurry red fury
down onto the stone
wall where the field
mouse was hiding,
then for missing, all
the more furious back up.

MEMORIES

I've had it with memories.
They don't interest me anymore.
Once they did.
That was years ago when there were fewer.
There are many more now.
They all come together dressed in dreams.

TO H. S.

I got your book today
and read it cover to
cover and smiled or
laughed or sighed but
didn't weep because
when I wanted to weep,
they said, "We forbid it,"
so please teach me how
you got them to do that.

GUNNERY PRACTICE AT WEST POINT

They're twenty miles away,
but I can hear what sounds
like thunder, what sounds
exactly like thunder from over
the mountains, the cadets
firing the big guns. Never having
been in war, I can say only
that they sound only like what
I've heard before, like thunder,
exactly like thunder from over
the mountains, from far away.

from **OLD** (2024)

SEEING ME SITTING

Seeing me sitting
outside waiting for my
financial advisor to stop
by to advise me of my
finances, the sun says,
"Solonche, you foolish
old man, here, come nap
upon my golden lap."

THE CRUELTY OF EXACTITUDE

It's the mind's right
to expect faultlessness.
"Picture it," it demands,
and although you can't,
try as you might,
you still will blame only your hands.

SUNDOWN

Go down the stairs at sundown.
Go down the road at sundown.
Go down the valley at sundown.
Go down to the oak tree at sundown.
Go down on your knees at sundown.
Go down to the depth of your silence at sundown.
Go down to the heart of your soul at sundown.

LONGING

I, too, know it in
my bones, feel it
bleed from my eyes,
the cruel blindness
worse than blindness,
the blindness that lets
you see that for which
you long and that alone.

PETUNIA

Tenacious, obstinate, stubborn,
purple on purpose more
than ever, the last petunia
in the pot leans over the exact spot
the sun was last afternoon.

OLD

Old and older than
and oldest among,
and the young (Bless
their hearts!) shall live
to regret all they say
about us.

IT'S GOOD TO BE OUTSIDE

It's good to be outside
again after days of rain
and cold and cold rain,
again in the warm air,
again governed by a
generous sun. How good
it is to be outside again
among the shadows
sharp on the walls,
sawing through the houses.

BETWEEN

It is after noon but still before dusk,
and the indecisive hours rub
off on my hands.

ZHAO LI

I paused to look at the swamp.
It was silent.
Oh, how I miss my old friend, Zhao Li,
who would read its lips
and tell me what it says.

TWO CLOUDS

Two clouds, white as a swan's
wings or an angel's, converge
from the left and the right on
the sun, which lights the clouds
from behind gloriously. Somewhere
someone is dropping to her knees
in prayer, and I, as much as I would
like to, can't blame her.

FOR R.A.

True, many may have
written better poems,
but not one asked
better questions than you.

VERY SHORT CONVERSATION
IN THE MONASTERY

Student: "Master,
what is the difference
between having
nothing on your
mind and having
your mind on nothing?"
Master: "Enlightenment."

ALL THINGS ASPIRE TO BE ROUND

The square wants to be round.
The triangle wants to be round.
The parallelogram wants to be round.
The octagon wants to be round.
The heart wants be round.
The soul wants to be round.
All want to be round to fit, when they die,
into heaven, which is round.

THE FUTURE IS FEMALE

"The future is female," you said,
Korkut, so I had to ask you why.
"The future is female because she
is a beautiful Spanish lady who
comes bringing bad news," you
said, so I smiled and nodded and
said, "Bring her on, that senorita,
that senora, for I am ready for her
beauty and for her beautiful bad news."

MAY PASTORAL

Hail to you, hummingbird, throated
with ruby, as you sip the sugar water!
Hail to you, jay, plumaged in the blue
of the sky, as you feast on the last suet of the year!
Hail to you, hairy woodpecker,
as you wait your turn on top of the crook there!
Hail to you, mourning dove,
as you softly coo unseen in the wood!
Hail to you, crow, as you carry the cross
of your shadow wherever you go!

A POT WITHOUT FLOWERS

The dirt waits to become
soil again, has waited months
in the potting shed's cool dark,
and now, in the sun for the first
time since November's failing sun,
begins to remember what it's for,
begins to anticipate the spade's
plunge, begins to prepare for
the nudging of the suckling roots.

CRIMSON AZALEA

Who expected this? I didn't,
not after last spring's resplendence,
not after such a voice, so full and
so sweet, with which you sang.
Oh, I hear you, old crimson azalea.
I, too, am getting old. Old brother,
I, too, am finding it harder and
harder to force a smile.

MYSTERIES

For example, I
followed a wasp
as it zigzagged
across the yard,
curious to see
where its nest was.
It was only one of
many mysteries today.

SATURDAY

Only men here so far
at the brewery. We two,
two there, two there, only
pairs of men, but it is early,
not yet two o'clock. They
talk about women, their
women, other women, all
women. We talk about
women, our women, other
women, all women. Women.

THERE IS A YELLOW

and white Dutch iris
in the garden where
there was never one before,
an interloper among the peonies,
which are just beginning to bow
down from the burden of their burgeoning
behind and to the left and to the right.

POEM BASED ON A LINE BY DONALD REVELL

I do not have a dog. I never had a dog.
What boy never had a dog? What teenager,
what young man, never mourned the loss
of his best friend in the world? I was that boy.
I was that teenager, that young man. I am
that old man. I cannot say that "Death calls
my dog by the wrong name." So I am grateful
to you, Donald Revell. I thank you for sharing your dog,
and I thank you for sharing your dignified disdain
        for death.

THE CHURCH

The church here is not pink
like yours, Bill, but white
like all the others, so I cannot
as you did compare it to "the
pink and rounded breasts
of a virgin!" but perhaps to
that same one in her white
wedding dress, tall, erect,
wooden, stock-still at the altar.

ANOTHER BUDDHIST

What is it that attracts
them so to him who
never wrote a poem,
at least none we know
about? Ah, yes, it's what
attracts them to the old
ponds, to the frogs jumping
in, to the plop of the water.

from **NIGHT VISIT** (2025)

NIGHT VISIT

There is supposed to be a city,
a city that comes out only at night,
not in dreams but in actuality
like a miracle, like the moon, like the stars,
but the city I see when I step outside
on a summer night is the city of the crickets.
Ah, is it not a pity that we are not in Andalucia?

THE CIVIL WAR

A Quaker Union
officer wrote to his
mother not to worry
because he didn't
kill anyone himself
but only ordered his
men to.

Q & A

"What do women want?"
 asked Freud.
"What does poetry want?"
 I ask.
"The same,"
 answers Freud.
"The same,"
 I answer.

ON MY BIRTHDAY

It was 1946.
It was the 16th of July.
It was 4:22 in the afternoon.
It was when I was born.
It changed my life.

THE STORE

Into the store came
a lovely mother
and her daughter
lovelier still as though
a mysterious wish
had been granted.

ROSES

Like you, Alfred, I, too,
"thought of the rose and its thorns,"
for once I had roses, red ones
with thorns, sharp ones that never
let me forget they were roses
and not lilies, roses and not irises,
roses and not marigolds. But oh, red
roses, you fickle lovers, I forgot,
I forget, and now I miss you to death.

ALL THE REST

Like you, Alfred, I, too, "never
played pool with all the rest."
I played only with my brother
and father in the pool hall on
Allerton, but I would glance over
at all the rest smoking the cigarettes,
drinking the beer, joking about the
skirts, and I wished I were of them,
one of all the rest playing pool.

NINA SIMONE

My neighbor, Harry, is 90. He needs hearing aids.
He says when two people are talking, he can hear
only the person with the higher voice. He says he
can't hear the person with the low voice, especially
if it's a woman with a low voice. That means he's
missing the smoky, sultry, sexy voices of the likes
of Lauren Bacall and Kathleen Turner and Nina
Simone. Oh, what a pity, of Nina Simone.

WHISKEY

Unlike you, Alfred, I
do not think that "Scotch is
reasonable," for I've heard
it said by an expert, a connoisseur,
an aficionado of all things whiskey,
how much "Scotch goes down
the way bourbon comes up."

WHERE

I saw it today, where
I want to be buried.
It's the cemetery next
to the apple orchard.
It doesn't have to be
this cemetery and this
orchard, as long as it's
a cemetery next to an
orchard, and as long as
I'm as close to the apple
trees as the local laws
allow, and if possible, closer.

from **BARREN ROAD** (2025)

FOUND POEM
OVERHEARD AT MY NEIGHBOR'S WAKE

Sorry, dear,
I'm not
feeling
this funeral.

THE AIR IS STILL

The air is still,
so still, one doubts
that it is even air
except that it can be
breathed in and held
and breathed out again
into the very spot it had been.

DANCE

I have two left
feet, so I dance
out of both sides
of my mouth.

DEMENTIA

So you want to know what this sleep is?
What this dream is?
You must think of the first sleep you slept
out of the womb.
You must think of your dream of the womb.
If you cannot, you will not know this sleep.
If you cannot, oh, my friends, you will not know
this dream.

FORSYTHIA

Leaving this overcast,
dark gray, rainy morning,
I heard the forsythia at
the bottom of the driveway
shout, "We blackmailed the sun
to be this sun-golden, so
do not forget this when you get
back, and it is here this afternoon."

THE CHANGE

How quick is the change.
Not a moment is wasted,
not an instant of sun not taken,
not a single degree unused,
how can we say *Already*
to these who have been
ready so long?

SHORT APRIL PASTORAL

The wind is winter's unfinished business.
The shoots of the lilies pay it no mind.
Soon we will know which trees are dead, which alive.
Soon the grass will cleanse our minds of snow.
The tallest trees make the best dancers.
Even the dead trees dance joyously.
The daffodils hog the yellow.
They have no need to dance, but they do.

THE ANGEL

Such a beautiful woman
in the supermarket,
surely she was an angel.
You cannot blame me, for
she was from that angle.

CONVERSATION ON EASTER AT EASTER

I asked him about suffering.
He said that philosophers
have struggled over it for
centuries. I asked him again
about suffering. He said that
it is needed for redemption.
I asked him again about
suffering. He said that men
bring it on themselves.
I stopped asking him about
suffering, for I saw that
he was suffering enough.

MOUNTAIN LAUREL

You are old now,
Old Mountain Man,
and you are tall now, too,
taller than I am,
and your small white
flowers fall in
foamy splashes of spittle
down your long bony legs.

AFTER THE READING

After the reading, the poet was asked,
"Why do you write?" "I write because
the silence is too much to bear," he answered.
I hope someone asks me the same question,
for I shall answer, "I write because the noise
is too much to bear."

A WIND

A wind neither too gentle
nor too strong, but a wind
just right to blow the cherry
blossom petals from the cherry tree
on the other side of the house
over the roof has done just that.

TWO LAKES

As lifeless as this page
on which nothing is yet
written, yet not dead
either, for life, so much life,
is stirring just beneath
the surface of the two lakes.

CEMETERY

It is old enough to make unreadable the oldest stone.
Soon it will no longer even be a cemetery.
What does soon mean?
Soon means when the iron fence is rusted totally away.
Soon means when the thick brambles forbid you
visitation there.
Soon means when it is out of sight.
Soon means when it is out of mind.

THE TREES

The tree I a year ago
thought dead is alive.
The tree I a year ago
thought alive is dead.
This may be the best of
all reasons to stop thinking.

DANDELIONS

If they weren't yellow,
as bright and as yellow
as any daffodil, more so
than some daffodils,
I would mow them down
with the grass like grass.

AWAKENING FROM DREAMS

It takes longer now.
It takes more sun at the window.
It takes the sun longer at the window now.
My dreams are stronger.
They are stronger than the world.
They are better than the world.
When I awaken from dreams,
I fall into a dreamless sleep.

HOPE

Not an end in itself
but the means to an
end desired, like wings
or a woman's name.
Don't believe everything
you read. This is hope.
Just this.

SUDDEN SHADOW

Crow, you scorn
me unlike your cousin's
Samuel's, so caw everywhere,
and you will subdue
this blue air.

FIRST

The first butterfly I've seen
so far this spring flies
among the myrtle and the dandelions,
not stopping, not pausing, but
knowing that not these are the keys
to its chemical heart,
disappears behind the shed.

KAFKA

I wish we had lived at
the same time just long
enough to have shared
letters, one from me to
you, Franz, and one from
you to me. Only that long.

THE SURPRISE

"I have a surprise for you,"
 says the morning.
"I do not like surprises," I say.
"I have one anyway," says the morning.
"Fine. What is it?" I say.
"You are alive," says the morning.

AT NO ONE'S GRAVE

This ground is undisturbed.
Here no digging has been done.
But death has been here.
It still is here. It has always been here.
It will always be here. With life,
together, inseparable. They are identical twins.
One male, one female.
No. Both female.

A GAME

Loud shouts at a game.
It does not matter
what. It is a game.
It is the home field.
The home team scores.
There are shouts.
The shouts are loud
from the field beyond
the trees as I go home
to my quiet house.

OLD

I know I am getting old.
Five pots for flowers
this year instead of eight.
Four types of flowers
in them instead of six.
Two whiskies at three
instead of three at five.
No women, no women,
no women instead of one.

PEONY

Peony I plucked out
from the garden space
to put in this vase,
it's your fault for being first.

READING

I get up and
put my book
on the chair.
It's out of place,
yet it waits
politely there.

DEMENTIA

"Does she still smile?"
her friend asked.
"Yes, she still smiles,"
I said. "I think she
will always smile,"
she said. "Yes, the doctor
thinks so, too, but the reasons
will change, he said," I said.

TO MY DAUGHTER

I do not wish a grave,
but you may give me one
if you insist. I cannot
stop you, for I know how
last wishes are many times
ignored when the living
believe the dead ask too much
of them, or much too little.

FOR E. K.

She has an eye for eyes,
this young artist,
still a teenager,
but look here,
how the mouths leave
much to be desired.

MONEY

I like money.
Emily Dickinson is my favorite poet.
For $32.35 I bought her *Complete Poems*.
For $49.99 I bought her *Complete Letters*.
For $50 in gas I visited her home
in Amherst, Massachusetts.
For $450,000 I could buy a lock of her hair on eBay.
I would like to if I had the money, the money I like.

UNCOLLECTED SHORT POEMS

I THINK THE PURE WHITE

I think the pure white
peonies are the saddest
of the peonies to watch
wilt, for they are the fair-
weather clouds of peonies
that melt to the dark muddy
brown the rain will make.

JACOB

I never dreamed
I wrestled with anyone
except myself, yet always
I awoke to enough
perspiration for two.

EVE

Eve had every right
to complain, but she
bit her tongue which
has been bleeding ever since.

YAHWEH

You left me no choice,
you know, you humans.
Free will was part of the plan
all along. What the hell
did you expect from one
who willed himself into
existence? From one who had
never been taught tautology?

ZHAO LI

Zhao LI is tired.
He does not
enjoy the red wine,
but now he enjoys
being tired.

ZHAO LI

Zhao Li writes his name and waits.
He waits and waits.
"Ah, now I see what I wait for,"
he laughs while crossing out his name.

ZHAO LI

Zhao Li pauses to look at a cloud.
It is a cloud that does not look
like anything else other than all other clouds.
This is why he pauses to look at it
before the wind causes it to look like
something other than all other clouds.

ZHAO LI

Zhao Li did not want to begin
writing in a new notebook,
but there was a new notebook
on the table, and there was a new pen
on the table, and there was a new pot of wine
on the table, and there was a new poem
in the new pot of wine,
so what was poor old Zhao Li to do?

THE RAIN STOPS

The rain stops so Zhao Li goes outside.
He takes a deep breath.
He takes another deep breath.
He takes a third deep breath.
"Ah, how fresh the world smells.
Ah, how new the world smells.
Ah, how innocent the world smells,"
he breathes. "Ah, what a cruel joke,"
Zhao Li laments, shaking his head.

BLACK

"Believe it, I am God's
favorite," it says. "I am
the eldest, the primordial
darkness, the one He sought
for solace when the others
nearly blinded him with light."

DEMENTIA

They are not gone,
the two great passions.
She sees the music now
and now hears the dance.

THE AFTERLIFE

The afterlife is
not mysterious.
It's the beforelife
only more serious.

A DRAGONFLY

A dragonfly, oblivious
to the moths and butterflies
above it, rests on the wall,
contented philosopher
who has found his stone.

WINE

"Yes, I know I'm no
good for you," it says.
"But admit it. You just
can't do without me,
can you? Never mind.
Never mind. Sleep now.
We'll talk in the morning."

POETRY

Frost can keep his
tennis and his net.
Give me the baseball
field and its foul lines.
And its foul lines.

STORM

It did not last long.
It did not need to.
It made the trees dance
to its tune and went on,
leaving in its wake
the hurt of barely a few branches
but then a clean, clear, fresh blue sky.
It was the life I would have liked to have lived.

GLASS

Most innocent of all
materials, what else
lets you see right through
it? What else? What else?

THE HORSES

If these horses were
the only ones on earth,
they would be all we
need to know about horses,
as they mind their business
in the paddock, grazing on
plenitude, looking up
only to ignore us again.

BOULDER

I see it every day at the edge
of my property, gray boulder
like the bald head of wisdom.
Sometimes I stare at it,   /
half-expecting it to speak,
to say something profound,
something stoical,
something as heavy as the ages,
something carved in stone.

TWO'S COMPANY

Scream of a Dying Star
was named one of the best
astronomy photographs
of 2024. At last, we have
the proof that we're not
alone in the universe.

TRUE SIMILE

There's a bee in
in the clover on
my lawn like a
bee in clover.

OLD PHOTOGRAPHS

I don't like old photographs.
Old photographs are cruel.
Old photographs are sadistic.
They enjoy inflicting pain.
Here is the perfect example on
the windowsill in front of me.
Look at the smile on my young
wife's face. And on my little
daughter's face, look at the laugh.

PHOTOSYNTHESIS

Has the green insect
on the screen spent so
much time in the grass
that it's learned its secret?

BOOKS

There are too many.
They should be pulped.
They should be pulped to make useful things.
Cardboard coffins, for instance.
I'd like to be buried in unread copies of *Moby Dick*.

FIST

The
hardest
way
to write.

SPITE

A long spit
with the eye.

THE LAKE

is beloved
of the sun,
its mirror
amid miles
of trees that
only take
and never
give back.

A CROW

flies back
and forth
across
the road.
Is this how
omens work?

SUICIDE

For once,
he stunned us.

OR NOT

Unlike you, Bill, I
do not dance naked
(or not) in my room,
north (or not), singing
(or not), but nevertheless,
like you, I am lonely,
born so (or not), I am
lonely, best so (or not),
happy (or not), at home
(or not) or not.

ALPHA AND OMEGA

The last does not know
anymore it is the last
than the first knows it
is the first, but of course,
I might be wrong on both counts.

ZHAO LI GOES OUTSIDE

to write but has forgotten
to bring paper. "Just as well.
I have also forgotten to bring
a poem," he laughs.

AGAIN ZHAO LI

goes outside to write,
and this time he remembers
to bring paper but now has
forgotten a pen. "Just as well.
I have also neglected the poem
I wanted to write yesterday,"
smiles Zhao Li without laughing.

MOVIE

It was long.
Probably too long.
Not the sort of movie
you would want to see
more than once.
It was based on true events.
Not the sort of true events
you would want to happen
more than once.

YESTERDAY

We're not yet done
with each other,
yesterday and I, for
there is one thing
more to forget.

CHINESE POEMS

I love looking at Chinese poems.
I love looking at Chinese poems more
than at any other poems.
I cannot read Chinese, so I have to say
that I look at them.
I love them because they are beautiful to look at
and since they all look the same to me,
they are all beautiful.
That they do not mean the same doesn't matter at all,
for they are all beautiful the same way,
like a strange and wonderful world inhabited only by roses.

YELLOW CHRYSANTHEMUMS

It should be the only
color allowed, this
bright sunlight yellow
for this afternoon
yellow sunlight on
all the porches in town.

I CANNOT SLEEP

I cannot sleep.
I go out.
I do not have to look up
to see that the stars fill every corner of the night.
The stars overwhelm me.
Homesickness overwhelms me.
"You must go back to where you came from," they say.
"Yes, yes," I say. "I must go back."
But for which one, for which one am I homesick?

THIS MORNING

At 7:15 this morning,
a crow calls ridicule
on the sky as it tries
on the full moon, which
is two sizes too small.

DUSK

On an ocean
of shadows,
the sun furls
its golden sail
but still follows
the wind west.

THE JOY OF LONELINESS

I was lonely.
I looked in the mirror
and knew the joy
of another's loneliness.
It was the loneliness of our joy.

VIEW OF A LAKE

Unobstructed save for
a split rail fence, more
invitation than obstruction,
and a swing set with slide
on which there are no
children, mysteriously,
on this sunny Sunday,
the lake spreads out in
a miracle of emptiness.

ZHAO LI FINISHES THE POEM
HE BEGAN 70 YEARS AGO

When I was 8 years old,
they told me I looked
like my mother. When
I was 28 years old, they
told me I looked like my
father. When I was 48
years old, they told me
I looked like my aunt.
When I was 68 years old,
they told me I looked like
my uncle. Now I am 78
years old. I look like myself.

DREAMS

When I awaken from sleep,
and, clear-eyed, I see my dream
for what it is, for who dreams it,
how can I not know that it is
the same dream time and time
again since I myself am, time
and time again, the same dreamer
who falls into the same sleep to dream it?

IRONY

It's not for me, not
anymore, not since out-
growing that wise guy's
plaything and letting
the convolutions, wrinkles,
creases of my mind go flat.

SHANGRI-LA

It is always a valley,
except the Garden
of Eden, which was
an oasis in a desert,
which was a mirage,
which a valley can never be.

A MYSTERY

I do not wear my glasses
when I sleep, yet I see
perfectly without them
in my dreams.

WAR

The war clears
to reveal the fog.
The fog clears
to reveal the smoke.
The smoke clears
to reveal the dead.
The dead clear
to reveal the future.
The future clears
to reveal the wars.

EMPTY FIELD IN WHICH THERE USED TO BE THREE HORSES

They are not a memory, for an
empty field cannot remember what
grazed on its grasses. What it remembers
is only that it can, for another year, grow
more grasses for grazing on or not.

VERY SHORT DECEMBER PASTORAL

The cold freezes
the snow in place.
The sun shines its
usual uselessness.

BAD MORNING

The sun comes up over the ocean of trees.
The songbirds have learned to sing the gulls' chanties.
Unsteady on my feet, I hold the banister
to keep from sliding on my way across on my way down
to the toilet on the stairs.

FULL

Full of the sun,
the full moon blinds
me with assumption.

NIGHTINGALE

The nightingale
is the national
bird of Ukraine.
My heart aches.

TRANSFIGURATION

It snowed but not enough
to bring the plows out
of the highway garage,
yet just enough for the world
to will itself transfigured
into something somehow
white from inside out.

BELIEF

For years I believed I was
the loneliest until I passed
a field with one old horse
and realized how wrong I was.

CHRISTMAS

How good to get
the gifts one wants,
those that one can
actually use, so
I thank you, madam,
for the Merlot
and for the Cabernet
Sauvignon.

CORRECTIONS

Another one to add
to the list.
Ah, is there is no
end to them?

ADOLPHE SAX

He died in obscurity,
penniless, the man
who gave us what I'm
listening to, the voice
of John Coltrane.

A WISH

I wish I lived within view
of a mountain, a tall
mountain capped in snow
all year long, a mountain
whose peak is sometimes
veiled by clouds, clouds
that move off at predictable
intervals to allow me to see
the mountain majestic in full
when I've had enough mystery.

ABOUT THE AUTHOR

Nominated for the National Book Award, the Eric Hoffer Book Award, and nominated three times for the Pulitzer Prize, J.R. Solonche is the author of more than forty books of poetry and coauthor of another. He lives in the Hudson Valley.

SHANTI ARTS

NATURE ▪ ART ▪ SPIRIT

Please visit us online
to browse our entire book catalog,
including poetry collections and fiction,
books on travel, nature, healing, art,
photography, and more.

Also take a look at our highly regarded art
and literary journal, *Still Point Arts Quarterly*,
which may be downloaded for free.

www.shantiarts.com